COACHING YOUTH CRICKET

COACHING YOUTH CRICKET

An Essential Guide for Coaches, Parents and Teachers

Luke Sellers

THE CROWOOD PRESS

First published in 2014 by
The Crowood Press Ltd
Ramsbury, Marlborough
Wiltshire SN8 2HR

www.crowood.com

British Library Cataloguing-in-Publication Data
A catalogue record for this book is available from the British Library.

ISBN 978 1 84797 794 6

Typeset by Servis Filmsetting Ltd, Stockport, Cheshire

Printed and bound in Singapore by Craft Print International

CONTENTS

Introduction   6

1   Player-Centred Coaching   7

2   Coaching Tools   14

3   Player Development   29

4   What Makes a Good Practice Session   34

5   Skills, Drills and Practices: Warm-Ups   39

6   Skills, Drills and Practices: Batting   45

7   Skills, Drills and Practices: Bowling   69

8   Skills, Drills and Practices: Fielding and Wicketkeeping   85

9   Skills, Drills and Practices: Games   115

10   Skills, Drills and Practices: Nets   121

11   Session Planning and Differentiation   125

12   Running a Team   129

13   Extras   136

     Appendix: ECB Guidelines   141

     Index   142

INTRODUCTION

Becoming a cricket coach is one of the most rewarding things I have done and continues to enthuse, surprise and inspire me. It is also a lot of fun.

The aim of this book isn't to tell you how to coach, it is simply to offer you some ideas to help you on your way. Whether you are a parent who is new to cricket and wanting to assist at your son's or daughter's weekly training session, or a qualified coach running your own team, this book aims to equip you with all the tools you need to feel confident.

With cricket's list of rules, idiosyncratic rules and variety of skills this can appear a daunting prospect – especially if you haven't played the game. But don't worry if you

don't know a legspinner from an inswinger, because everything you need to know for coaching youth cricket, from top tips on technique to advice on managing match days, can be found in this book. Aimed at coaches working with children aged between seven and thirteen, the ideas, advice and practices in this book are designed to complement and enhance your own existing skills and coaching philosophy.

By giving your time to developing the next generation of cricketers you are a vital asset to your club, school or representative team. I hope you find coaching cricket a fulfilling and enjoyable experience, and I wish you all the very best of luck with it!

USING THIS BOOK

As this book is for coaches working with players aged from around seven to thirteen, the practices are designed to cover a wide range of abilities. To try to make sure the drills are relevant to coaches across these ages, the majority are aimed at players somewhere in the middle of this age range, for example under elevens. However, every drill contains ideas of how to make it harder, to make it suitable for older players, and ways to make it easier, to make it suitable for younger players. For an idea of what skills are most suited to your age group, see Chapter 11.

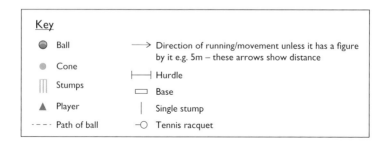

Key

- 🔴 Ball
- 🔵 Cone
- ⫴ Stumps
- ▲ Player
- - - - Path of ball

- ⟶ Direction of running/movement unless it has a figure by it e.g. 5m – these arrows show distance
- ⊢⊣ Hurdle
- ⬭ Base
- | Single stump
- ─○ Tennis racquet

CHAPTER I

PLAYER-CENTRED COACHING

A common mistake among those who work in sport is spending a disproportional amount of time on 'x's and o's' as compared to time spent learning about people.

Mike Krzyzewski, Basketball

What is Player-Centred Coaching?

Player-centred coaching is the idea of putting the player at the heart of the coaching process. It is the starting point for the England and Wales Cricket Board's (ECB) coach education courses, and is widely recognized across all sports as the underpinning theme of quality coaching. Although the needs of their groups will be very different, the method is just as relevant for coaches working with young players in a club environment as it is for those working with professionals at an élite level.

Outlining the benefits of the approach in their influential book *Athlete-Centred Coaching: Developing Inspired and Inspiring People*, Lynn Kidman, Rod Thorpe and David Hadfield suggest that a player-centred approach improves motivation and understanding and helps prepare players for competition:

Some of the main advantages of using an athlete-centred approach to coaching are that athletes are motivated to learn, and they have a greater understanding and retention of both tactics and skills. . .

This approach is clearly beneficial given that athletes must be self-sufficient in their performance, decision-taking and option-taking while participating in their respective sport.

To start to think about the approach in practice and the benefits it might have, here is a quick-fire list of questions to think about in relation to a typical coaching session:

- Who is the most important person in the coaching session?
- Whose goals and ambitions should drive the session?
- Who provides the answers and sets the challenges during the session?
- Who is responsible for learning and skill development during the session?

Traditionally the answer to some or all of these questions may have been 'the coach', but if they are that central to a session, there is a danger they may be putting themselves ahead of the needs of their players. Although this method may provide a short-term 'fix' for their players it is unlikely to bear fruit in the long term. Even if the coach is hugely knowledgeable about the game, this will be wasted if their players don't buy into it. For example, if a coach decides to have a session on running between the wickets when their squad feel they already do this well, the players are unlikely to be motivated by the practice. This in turn causes them to lose motivation and closes their mind to the possibility of learning new skills, and the result is that the practice is unlikely to be a success. If a coach can instead make their players central to the coaching process and encourage them to drive their own learning, then the opposite is true.

If we think about the questions above again and accept that the answer to each of them is 'the player(s)', then the benefits that Kidman *et al* talk about become obvious:

- If the players are viewed as the most important people in the coaching process, then the coach can tailor a session to their exact needs. In turn this provides them with the ideal environment for successful practice.
- If the session is driven by the players' goals they are more likely to remain motivated during a session and select achievable outcomes.
- In a match players must be able to think for themselves. By having to problem solve during a practice session they are replicating the decision-making process they will face on the pitch.
- A player-centred method puts the player in charge of their own learning, which increases the chance of them retaining new skills and 'buying in' to what the coach has to say.

So, if we accept that a player-centred approach is an integral part of modern-day coaching, the next question is, how do we put it into practice?

Using a Player-Centred Approach

At first glance it may appear that putting the players at the centre of your coaching

and encouraging them to drive their own development diminishes the role of the coach. But while making your players more self-sufficient is a desirable outcome, nothing could be further from the truth.

While it is called 'player-centred coaching', the reality is that it is built around a trusting two-way relationship between coach and player. It requires the coach to gain an in-depth understanding of the individuals in their group, from their level of ability to what motivates them to play cricket. Having gathered this information, the next challenge for a coach is to use it to plan and deliver practice sessions that meet their players' specific needs.

For many of us brought up on prescriptive, one-size-fits-all PE lessons at school, this may seem like a daunting prospect. But even if the term is new, you will almost certainly be running practices and drills that are at least partly player-centred already. The challenge is to take this a step further and try to deliver sessions that cater for the needs of all the individuals in your session and are driven by the players themselves.

To ensure your next session is truly player-centred, begin by asking yourself a few simple questions about your group and the outcomes you hope to achieve.

Who are you coaching?

The first and most important part of player-centred coaching is to get to know your players. This will allow you to understand their needs and to build your sessions around them. In an ideal scenario you would hope to have a detailed picture of your players before you begin coaching, but if this isn't possible try to find out the following things at the earliest opportunity:

- What are the names of the players?
- How old are they?

It's important to get to know your players at the earliest opportunity.

- What is their level of cricketing experience and current skill level?
- What are their strengths, and what are the areas to improve?
- What do they want/need to learn?
- Do they have any injuries, or are there any other factors that will impede their ability to learn?

What outcomes are you looking for?

Having got to know your players, the next stage is to work out what outcomes you will help them achieve. These could be cricket skills, physical movements, tactical thinking or mental attributes you hope to see from your players during a session. The outcomes should be identified using the knowledge you have gained about the group and should also be agreed in partnership with the players. For example, there is no point setting goals for your players if they are not motivated to achieve them, or think they are too easy or hard. Instead, involve them in the process by asking them what they think they can achieve. After all, the best and most important judge of their individual success is the player themselves.

When identifying the outcomes for a session ask yourself the following:

- Which part of the game are we looking to develop? For example, technical, tactical, physical or mental
- Which specific cricket skill will we use? For example, front-foot drive, bowling action, overarm throw, and so on
- Which part of the skill will we focus on? For example, staying balanced at the crease, grip, transferring weight towards the target, and so on
- What will success look like by the end of the session?

The last one is, of course, by far the most difficult one to answer, and it may change during the session. At different times you may find that your players' achievements exceed your expectations; at other times they may fall short of what you expect.

The more you learn about your players, the better you will become at predicting the likely outcomes. The same is also true for your players – the more they become used to sessions that involve them setting their own goals, the more realistic and achievable they will become.

Types of Practice and Coaching Tools

By building up a picture of your players and identifying the outcomes you hope to achieve, you are now in a position to plan an effective player-centred session. In order to meet the needs of the group you will need to work out the best methods of practice, the type of equipment you will use, and what you, as a coach, will do to help facilitate learning. All of these decisions should be made with your specific players in mind.

As a coach you will have your own preferred coaching style, drills and equipment. And while it is valuable to recognize your own strengths and weaknesses, it is important that these do not overshadow the needs of your players. A good coach has the ability to adapt to the needs of whichever group they are working with.

Before starting the session think about the following questions:

- What type of practice will I use? For example, will I use a small-sided game, nets or match scenario?
- What equipment will I use?

- What coaching tools will I use? For example demonstrate, observe, question
- How will I measure success?

Player-centred approach in Practice

Coaching in different settings will provide a variety of challenges for coaches attempting to use a player-centred approach. In a one-to-one session with a player with whom you have worked regularly it should be fairly straightforward to create a practice environment that you know will help them to achieve success. But if you are presented with a squad of twenty under-eleven players you have never seen before, the challenge of being player-centred is much greater.

Here is one way to gain enough information in ten to fifteen minutes to run an excellent player-centred session for a group of young players. The practice below would work well with players from as young as seven up to eleven. The beauty of this method is that the players are active and engaged the whole time rather than sitting having a conversation for ten minutes, which they may find a little dull.

After introducing yourself to the group, set up a simple game of non-stop cricket (see Chapter 9 for the basic set-up). In addition to the normal non-stop cricket rules I would add in a few different elements in order to help you observe not just a variety of different technical skills, but also tactical thinking and physical and mental characteristics:

- In order to observe the accuracy of the players' throwing, make a box from cones where the bowler has to stand. The bowler cannot leave this box, and therefore there is little margin for error for the fielders.
- Place three 'goals' made from cones, one at cover, one straight and the third at square leg. Batsmen are awarded four extra runs if they hit the ball through the goal.
- Finally give the batsmen the chance to use a cricket bat, tennis racket or a single stump. Batsmen using the bat score runs normally, those using the tennis racquet only score half the normal runs, while players using the single stump score double runs per shot.
- In this practice it can be useful to have the coach as the bowler so you can vary feeds accordingly. To ensure the game doesn't take too long, limit it to a maximum of four balls each.

By setting the game up and running it in this way you will be able to observe a number of different things:

Technical: During the game you will be able to see the players' throwing, catching and ground-fielding skills. You can also view the batsmen's grip and stance. And by varying the feed you can find out which players are able to play the front-foot drive and defensive shots.

Tactical: The game allows you to see a player's ability to judge a run, to see who looked for the gaps (goals), and also the fielders' ability to work as a team to retrieve the ball.

Physical: As it is a highly active game you can observe the players' fundamental movement skills (such as agility, balance, co-ordination and speed). For example you can see their speed and agility as they run between the wickets and in the field. You can also see their co-ordination and balance when they are throwing and striking the ball.

Mental: By noticing which bat the players choose to use you will get a sense of which members of the group are the more confident, which are more cautious, and which are risk takers.

Although traditionally we may use a game at the end of a session rather than at the beginning, here you can see its value in helping you learn about your players. After just ten to fifteen minutes you will be armed with enough information about the group to be able to identify their strengths, the areas they need to improve, and the different levels of ability within the group.

By asking questions about the game afterwards you will encourage your players to reflect on the game and help them identify the strengths and weaknesses that you have just observed. For example, during the game a number of players may have been caught out. By asking them what was the most common way of getting out and how this could be avoided, the players will provide the coach with the perfect theme for the coaching session that follows.

Using the players' feedback and your own observations from the game, you will now have the knowledge to set up a batting practice with the appropriate level of challenge for the players in the group. As they have been involved in identifying the area they are going to work on – hitting the ball along the ground – rather than being 'told' by the coach, they are also more likely to 'buy into' the session.

Clearly, to use the method above a coach needs good observation and analysis skills, but it is a great example of how to learn enough about your players quickly in order to deliver a session built around their needs, even without prior knowledge of the group.

A non-player centred approach

I once worked at an indoor cricket school that used to run a lot of one-to-one coaching sessions. On a typical Saturday morning each coach would work with four or five different players for an hour at a time. These could range in age from six to sixty, and from beginners to talented county youth players and club cricketers.

One of the major challenges of these sessions as a coach was that you often didn't know anything about the player until they arrived. This meant that in a very short period of time you had to find out their age, experience, skill level and goals, and come up with a suitable session. This initial – and hugely important – conversation with a player often took place with the parents watching, and you frequently had the sense that they felt they hadn't paid good money to have you standing around 'chatting' to their son or daughter.

One morning I became conscious that the coach in the net next door was starting his sessions a lot more quickly than me. Anxious to try and get my players active earlier and to ensure their parents felt they were getting value for money, I asked him what his secret was. He told me that he was going to run the same session with every player who turned up that morning, which saved a lot of time as he didn't need to talk to the player for long, and didn't need to change his plans or equipment. When I questioned this approach he told me that the session he was running – a batting drill involving the front foot drive and a bowling machine – was a good practice for everyone as it reinforced the basics. While I am not suggesting that the coach's motives weren't positive, it is clear that such an approach was not player-centred.

Over the course of the morning I watched the coach run three more identical sessions with three individuals of differing abilities aged between nine and sixteen. And naturally as a result the three sessions had very different levels of success. The first player I observed – a district standard batsman aged around thirteen – coped well with the practice, achieved plenty of success, and appeared to enjoy the session. The second – the older player – kept hitting the ball in the air despite being repeatedly told not to by the coach. When the coach finally asked the player why he wasn't keeping the ball on the ground, he said it was because he had done a similar drill last session and wanted to move on to hitting over the top. Essentially he was bored because he didn't want to do the drill, and the result was that his lack of motivation had a negative effect on its outcome.

By this time there were only ten minutes left in the session, and the coach said that if the player knuckled down and completed the drill he would be able to look at hitting over the top in the next session. The player accepted this, but did not appear particularly happy or motivated. The third player – the youngest – struggled to play the front-foot drive as the ball was bouncing too high from the bowling machine. The longer the session went on, the more he became frustrated, until eventually the coach changed his plan and switched to underarm feeds. Unfortunately by this time the player had become so frustrated that he wasn't focusing on the task and became slightly tearful as he continually failed to achieve success.

It was clear that by not taking the time to get to know his players the coach had failed to meet the needs of at least two of them. As a result both of these players left the centre feeling unhappy and demotivated.

As a young coach at the time I didn't feel confident enough to speak to the other coach at the end of the session to share my reservations over his approach. However, what I observed did reinforce my belief in the importance of player-centred coaching, and I have since always tried to make sure I take the time to find out as much as I can about my players at the start of a session.

CHAPTER 2

COACHING TOOLS

Coaching cricket – as with other sports – is an art rather than an exact science, otherwise we would all do it the same way and achieve identical outcomes. But this is clearly not the case. If you look at successful coaches and managers across any sport you will find an infinite number of personalities, styles and methods. From quiet analytical types such as India coach Duncan Fletcher to high-energy innovators such as England's Peter Moores, there are many ways to achieve success.

In your own coaching or playing you will have come across numerous excellent coaches who operate in very different ways. However, while everyone will have a slightly different style and approach, there are many traits, methods and beliefs that they will have in common. These may relate to the types of practice a coach favours, or the way they behave in order to get key messages across to their players.

In this chapter we will separate these two areas and look at the different 'coaching tools' that coaches use to promote learning in their sessions. From the ability to observe and analyse technique, provide demonstrations or ask questions, there are a number of 'coaching tools' that most good coaches have at their disposal. Mastering some, or all of these in isolation will not instantly make you a fantastic coach: instead the process is much more like baking a cake. If a successful session is the cake itself, then the coaching tools are the ingredients and techniques you use to create it. A good baker will need to know the exact amounts of each ingredient to add, and the techniques required to turn them into the perfect cake. Too much of one ingredient, or too little stirring of the mixture could have a hugely detrimental effect on the outcome.

The challenge for the coach as compared to the baker is that while the process for baking a cake remains the same each time, the ingredients of a good coaching session change because you are dealing with the unpredictability of human beings rather than flour and eggs.

One of the skills of a coach is knowing the right tools to use at the right time with the right players. Below are examples of some of the key coaching tools that every coach should have in their armoury. While I have used examples that often follow one another choronologically, there is no set order to use them in.

Some tools, like giving clear instructions, are likely to be a regular starting point for a session, but they may also be used at other times. Some coaches may want to start with a demonstration, while for others the first thing they do will be to observe and analyse the group. The tools you use, and the order and frequency you use them in, will depend on you as a coach, the type of practice, and most importantly, the needs of the players.

Give Clear Instructions

Providing clear, simple instructions is important whoever you are coaching, but particularly when working with children. A concise explanation of a practice should tell the players exactly what you want them to do, why you want them to do it, and what the outcome should be. If your players do not understand what you are asking them to do, then the whole practice is likely to break down and you will be back to square one.

Below are a few tips for giving clear instructions.

Make sure you are positioned so every player can see and hear you

If you don't have eye contact from a player, then the chances are they are not listening and will not understand the task. Getting players to stand and sit in a line in a sports hall or between two cones out on the field can be an effective way of ensuring they are ready to listen.

Make sure that all players in the group can see and hear you.

Keep it short and simple – two minutes and your time is up!

Most people have a limited attention span, and this is especially true with children. From the time you start your explanation the clock is ticking, and the longer you keep talking the less likely your players are to be listening. Try to make sure that your instructions take no longer than two minutes. If they do, the likelihood is that you are talking too much or your practice is too complicated to explain in one go.

It is also important that the language you use is simple and appropriate for the age group you are working with. Cricket is full of terms that make no sense unless you are aware of their context within the sport. So before you start talking about googlys, gullies, throwing arms and the off-side, make sure your players know what you are talking about.

Where possible use a picture to help

People learn in lots of different ways, and for some, sitting and listening to someone talk is quite difficult. In order to help cater for different learners within your group, try to use a picture to illustrate your explanation. This could be as simple as having the practice set up in front of them, so you can point things out as you talk. These days it could also include showing them a practice on your iPad, or carrying a white board around with you (small ones are commercially available).

Use your voice

When I first started coaching I thought that I had to be loud and ultra-enthusiastic – like a children's television presenter – to get my messages across, but in fact the opposite is true. While it helps to have a loud, clear voice, some of the best children's coaches I have seen go the other way and reduce their volume when working with younger people.

By speaking clearly but quietly you draw your players in, which makes them listen. It also has the added bonus that any disturbance from them becomes clear and can be dealt with straightaway. There will, of course, be times when you need to be louder, and I would encourage you to experiment with how you use your voice when coaching.

It is also important to ensure you keep facing your players, and stay nearby while you are giving your explanation. I have seen many coaches make the mistake of running off to a corner of the practice station, or moving players to their starting positions for the drill while they are still talking to the group.

Use questions: check that your players understand before sending them away

How do you know if your players have understood your instructions? One way is to send them out to start the practice and see if chaos or a quality coaching session ensues. The other is to simply ask them.

Once you have given your explanation, ask your players simple questions to check they understand. Where are you going to stand? Who do you throw the ball to? How many points for an accurate throw? Where will your fingers point when you take the catch? By asking questions on any aspect of a practice you should get an accurate idea of whether your explanation has been understood. If working with younger children you can also make this exchange fun by offering points for correct answers.

Provide a Demonstration

The old adage about a picture being worth a thousand words can certainly ring true when it comes to trying to describe a technical skill in cricket. To get round the difficulties

CLEAR INSTRUCTIONS IN ACTION

Here is an example of how to provide clear instructions for the hit the stumps game. In this scenario the equipment has already been set up. I have deliberately left out coaching points, as this would make the explanation too long. Instead I would watch the group and bring in relevant coaching points later, as required.

Coach: 'Good morning everyone, today we are going to play the hit the stumps game – this is a fun team game that uses the overarm throw. Can you tell me when we might use the overarm throw in a game of cricket?'

Players: 'If we were trying to stop the batsman getting runs or going for a run-out.'

Coach: 'Fantastic answer. In this game we will be trying to hit the stumps as if we were going for a run-out.
   'Here are the rules. First I will divide you into two teams. If I give you a number one you are in team one. If I give you a two you are in team two.'
   (Attribute numbers alternately, and get the players to stand in their teams.)
   'Team one, you will start behind the line of blue cones (already laid out in view of the players), team two behind the line of red cones. You will have a ball each. When I shout "go" your aim is to try and knock over the wickets using a powerful overarm throw. If you knock over one set of wickets your team gets one point. We carry on until all the wickets have fallen over. The winning team will be the one who knocks the most down. The only rule is that you need to stay behind your line of cones at all times. I will make sure any spare balls come back to you.
   'Team one can someone tell me where you will stand?'

Player: 'Behind the blue cones.'

Coach: 'Team two, where will you stand?'

Player: 'Behind the red cones.'

Coach: 'How do you score a point?'

Player: 'By knocking the wickets over.'

Coach: 'And finally what is our one rule?'

Player: 'We have to stay behind the cones.'

Coach: 'Great, does anyone have any questions? OK, take up your positions. We will start as soon as I shout "go".'

of trying to explain complex physical movements, coaches have long preferred to offer a visual aid in the shape of a demonstration. A good demo is not only a valuable tool for simplifying explanations, it can also provide a spark of excitement that encourages players to want to learn a new technique. Giving players a picture also aids those in the group who are visual learners.

Below are five top tips for providing a quality demonstration.

Make sure everyone can see – two angles are better than one

It may seem obvious, but I have seen plenty of coaches offer perfect technical demonstrations that were almost entirely wasted as their players weren't positioned so they could all see. Before performing your demonstration think about what you want your players to focus on, and make sure they are in the optimum spot to see this.

Many cricket techniques will need to be viewed from more than one angle for the players to get a full idea of what you are asking them to do. Even with something simple such as the close catch there are certain things you will see from side on – for example, where the ball is taken in relation to the head, bending of the knees, etc. – that you wouldn't see as clearly from front on.

Even if you do the demonstration of your life on your first attempt it is always wise to perform the skill more than once. Often there will be a lot for players to take in, and it is virtually impossible to do this after a single demo. Make sure that you show them the skill at least two or three times from each angle.

Involve your players

Demonstrations are often seen as a one-way method of communication where the coach tells and shows the group what they want while the players listen passively. But this needn't be the case. The best coaches make sure that their players are actively involved in the demo process by asking them to focus on certain areas of the technique, and by questioning them afterwards. By drawing out the key coaching points in this way the players need to pay attention and are engaged in the process.

This has the added benefit of getting your players to begin analysing technique – something that will prove useful as they develop and begin reflecting on their own skills.

Keep quiet – let your demo do the talking!

Many coaches think it helps make things clearer to explain a technical skill as they perform it, but the opposite is true. If a player already has to focus on a complex skill – the pull shot, for example – trying to make sense of what a coach is saying at the same time will only confuse them. As a coach you should have the confidence to let your demo speak for itself. If you have set up the process by asking your players to focus on certain areas and they have performed the skill well, several times and from different angles, you won't need to say a word.

Demo with and without a ball

When providing a demonstration it can be useful to perform the skill both with a ball (live) and without a ball (shadow). The benefits of a live demo are that it can spark excitement among your players and make them want to learn a skill. The sight of a coach smashing a front foot drive or knocking the stumps over with a powerful overarm throw is guaranteed to grab your players' attention.

The downside to a 'live' demo is that the players may become distracted by the ball and may not focus on the coaching points you want them to. The other thing to consider is that a 'live demo' can go wrong. If you require a player to feed the ball to you, make sure you pick someone who is reliable, and tell them exactly what you want beforehand to ensure that you are able to perform the skill effectively.

Make sure you show your players the best possible picture – even if it isn't you

The goal of your demonstration should be to show your players the best possible example of a skill. While as coaches we should all aspire to offer top-notch demos, we also need to be aware that we may not always be able to perform a technique to the standard required.

If this is the case – for example, if you are a fast bowler trying to demonstrate wicketkeeping – it may be better to use a player (in this case the wicketkeeper!) from your group. There is nothing wrong with doing this providing the player is comfortable performing the skill in front of the group, and can do so to the required level.

You also need to make sure that if you regularly use players for demos you don't always use the same one, as this could cause problems within the group. These days it is also possible to show your players demonstrations in the form of video footage on your laptop or tablet.

It's a good idea to show techniques from more than one angle. Don't be afraid to use players to help if they can demonstrate better than you.

THE DEMONSTRATION PROCESS IN ACTION

The process below can be applied to any skill you are demonstrating. Here is an example of how it might work for the close catch.

- Introduce the skill and ask players where they think it would be used in a match.
- Divide the group into two, asking one half to focus on your hands and the top half of your body, and the other to look at your legs and feet.
- Making sure all your players can see you, perform the close-catch technique twice front on and twice side on.
- Using questioning, draw out what the players have observed. This should include some or all of the following: fingers pointing down, feet at least shoulders-width apart, knees bent, catching the ball underneath the eyes, 'giving' with the hands to cushion impact.
- Pick one or two of these points for players to focus on when they practise – for example, fingers pointing down and feet at least shoulders-width apart.
- Finish with a live demo – at least one from each angle so they can see the skill in action.

Observe and Analyse

Although it may seem straightforward, the ability to watch what is happening in a session and make sense of it is one of the hardest skills in coaching. It is also one of the most important, because without the ability to observe and analyse, it is impossible to know whether your players are achieving success or require extra assistance to do so. The other thing about observation and analysis is that it can be contentious. Everybody sees things slightly differently, and often the analysis of sporting skills can bring out strong opinions.

As a coach you will need to become adept at observing how your players are performing as a group and as individuals. Below are five top tips for observing and analysing a coaching session:

Take your time and look from different positions

Once they have set up a coaching session, some coaches feel they need to get actively involved in a practice straightaway. This is particularly true if they are coaching on a club training night in front of the players' parents. But unless something is clearly unsafe and in danger of causing an injury it is often more valuable to take a step back and observe what is going on. Coaches should move around the group so they can view different individuals and watch from different angles.

It is also important to watch players perform skills several times. Just because you see something happen once doesn't mean it is necessarily going to happen again – whether good or bad. Once you have taken the time to observe what is happening in a session you will be able to make an informed decision as to what you need to do next.

What am I observing?

When you are observing a session take the time to think about what you are looking at and also what you are looking for. This means thinking about the make-up of the players involved (their age, skill level and so on) and the outcome of the practice. The following

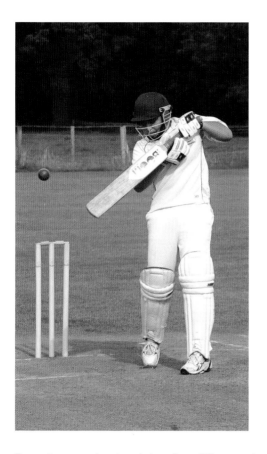 

Try to observe a player's technique from different angles.

questions may be useful in guiding your observations:

- Who are my players?
- What is the intended outcome of the exercise?
- Are they achieving that outcome?
- If not, then what outcome are they achieving?
- Is the method they are using safe?

The answers to these questions will help shape your analysis of the situation and inform you of what you do next.

Analyse: why are my players being successful/unsuccessful?

After observing your players and the outcome of what they are doing, the next step is to ask yourself why they are being successful or unsuccessful. This is crucial in informing you as to what you do with them next. In both cases there could be a variety of factors at play. As coaches we tend to focus on a player's technique, but we also need to evaluate their tactical, physical and mental skills.

You should also consider how the practice and the coaching tools you have employed have influenced what you have observed.

21

When analysing your players it is useful to have an image in your head of what the practice would look like if it were performed by an élite player: you can then compare this 'perfect' mental picture with what you are observing . By analysing the things that match and the things that don't you will build up an idea of what players are doing well and the areas they need to improve.

However, it is vital that this picture also includes the outcome as well. If the player is successful and their technique isn't going to cause injury, it doesn't matter if it doesn't conform with a 'perfect technical model' – there should be room for individuality.

Have a system

Although I have broken them down to aid understanding, observation and analysis naturally happen at the same time. While you are watching a skill you will automatically be judging whether it is effective and considering the reasons why. In addition to the process described above it is also useful to have a system to follow, as this will help you to follow a logical process and ensure you don't miss anything.

How you do this is up to you. Some coaches will observe and analyse a skill from a player's feet upwards, and others from the head down; some will work chronologically through a movement, while others start with the outcome and work backwards. You may well have your own entirely different method that works for you. If you are not sure of the best way to go about it I suggest trying a few different methods until you find one that you are happy with.

Decide what action to take

After observing and analysing a player, you will be left with a decision to make as to what you do next. This could include one or more of the following:

- Do nothing and let the practice continue.
- Reinforce the positives (matches) through praise.
- Intervene and try to help them improve (in the case of a mismatch). This could include offering the player simple instructions, asking questions or showing them a demonstration.
- Adapt the practice to the player's specific needs – this could involve making it harder or easier.

Providing Feedback

Once you have observed and analysed your player, the next step is to decide what to do with the information. In most instances you will probably want to discuss it with them, and the way that you give this feedback is crucial if it is to benefit your player and help them develop. Good, clear information delivered in the right way can be a real catalyst in helping them improve. Equally feedback that is ill-informed, confusing or negative can cause a player to become de-motivated, frustrated and unhappy.

Below are five top tips for providing feedback to your players.

Timing

As coaches we all like to step in and offer our advice, but there may be times when this isn't the right course of action. If your players are fully engaged in a practice you may not want to interrupt the flow of the session. It could be that you see evidence that the players are problem solving for themselves as they go along. In these instances the most productive thing you can do as a coach is let them carry on uninterrupted. At other times – such as if a player is at risk of causing themselves an injury – you may need to step in immediately.

ANALYSIS IN ACTION

Here is an example of the simple instructions and use of questions that you might employ when observing and analysing a basic target bowling practice.

Stage 1: After setting up and explaining the practice, move around so you can observe everyone. To observe bowlers in detail it is useful to watch from three angles: behind the bowler's arm and from behind their target (ensuring you are safe and don't interfere with the practice), and from the side. When watching from the side for a right-handed bowler you should position yourself on the leg side roughly level with the stumps but a few metres back. Remember to watch each bowler more than once.

Stage 2: As the practice is going on you need to consider your players and their outcomes. In this instance the players are an under-eleven group. All of them have played hard-ball cricket and can bowl overarm, but they are of mixed ability. The aim of the practice is for them to land the ball in a target zone roughly 1 × 1m on a good length. Within the group most players are achieving it some of the time, while a few are achieving it regularly. All of them appear to be using a safe technique.

Stage 3: When analysing their individual bowling techniques I am watching from the start of their run-up and comparing this with a 'perfect technical model' as I go through. For example:

- Player A's run-up is smooth, rhythmical and takes them towards their target (match).
- They take off on their left foot (for a right-handed bowler) and land on their right (match).
- They look outside their front arm at the target (match).
- Their head falls away to the off side at the point of delivery (mismatch).
- Their grip is orthodox for a seam bowler (match).
- Their follow-through takes them on a sharp angle away from their target to the off side (mismatch).
- The outcome is inconsistent, with the ball frequently going down the leg side (mismatch).

Stage 4: Following your analysis you are faced with a number of matches and mismatches. Arguably the most important of these is the last one – the outcome of the skill. The challenge now is to work out which of the mismatches is the root cause of the problem. Often in techniques one mismatch will be responsible for a chain reaction of others. In this instance it appears that the player's head position at the point of delivery is throwing him off balance resulting in the inconsistent outcome.

Stage 5: You are now have to decide what action to take, if any. Although this will be influenced by your conversations with the player (see Providing Feedback in the main text) it is possible to draw your own conclusions from what you have seen. For example, because the player's outcome is inconsistent you may want to try and help them stay more balanced at the point of delivery. If they manage to do this the mismatches in their follow-through and outcome are likely to be eradicated.

Providing the right feedback is crucial in players' development.

If a player is becoming frustrated at their lack of success in practice this may also cause you to step in sooner.

You should also consider if you want to give your feedback to a player one-to-one out of earshot from the rest of the group, or whether it can be done in front of others.

Ask the player what they think

If you have decided to share your observations with your player the first thing you should do is ask them what they think (and listen to their answers!). This will help them develop the ability to analyse their own game and take ownership of their learning. This also avoids provoking the negative feelings that can arise if a coach simply tells a player what they think he or she is doing wrong. Instead, ask them what they have noticed about their outcomes – for intance, their front foot drive keeps going in the air. You can then follow this up by asking why they think this is happening and what they think they can do to improve it.

The more you do this with the players the more comfortable they will be with the process, and the better their answers are likely to be. Remember that the overall goal for the coach is to encourage players to be self-sufficient, thinking cricketers who can problem solve for themselves.

Keep it simple – only tell them what they need to know

Whether you are helping the player find their own answers through questioning, offering your own advice, or a combination of the two, it is important to keep things simple. At the end of your exchange with a player they should know, firstly, what their current outcome is and why it is happening; and secondly, what they want their outcome to be and how they are going to achieve it.

For example, I am currently hitting the front foot drive in the air on a regular basis. This is because my head is leaning backwards at the point of contact. I want to try and hit the ball along the floor, and to do this I need to have my head over the ball at the point of contact. Any additional information to the points above is liable to overload and confuse the player. As a coach you will have observed and analysed a huge amount of information to get to this point, but much of this is not relevant to the player. Your job is not to tell the player *how much* you know but simply to tell them what they *need* to know.

Reinforce the positives

We tend to think of the observation and analysis process as being all about looking to correct perceived weaknesses, but this shouldn't be the case. Providing your players with positive feedback is just as important. Even if you are looking to help a player improve something, you should still make sure you praise them for the things they are doing well.

When praising players, try to offer a little extra information rather than just a simple 'well done'. For the praise to have a real impact make sure the player knows what they have done well and how they have done it. For example, in an overarm throw practice, rather than just saying 'well done' when a player hits the stumps, try to add value: for example, 'Well done on hitting the stumps, you were in a well balanced position and your front arm was pointing straight at the target.' You should also make sure that you reward effort as well as ability – and be careful not to focus all your praise on the same players.

Try not to use judgmental language

As coaches we are always making judgments on what we see. If you sit watching a game of cricket you will overhear people shouting 'great shot' or muttering 'that was a terrible ball'. But there are a number of problems with this. Firstly, these remarks are subjective and not necessarily rooted in fact. Is it a 'bad' shot if a player hits a technically perfect cover drive that is stopped by a fielder? Is it a good shot if the same player hits a boundary with a lofted-on drive that they were attempting to hit along the ground past the bowler? These questions open a potential minefield when we come to providing feedback for our players.

Where possible, try to get away from describing techniques as 'good' or 'bad', and focus on what you actually saw. Instead of telling your player that they used 'poor' foot movement for a shot, tell them what you saw: for example, 'I observed that when you played the pull shot your back foot didn't move.' By providing information in this way you give your players a more detailed picture of what they are doing. The other benefit is that by taking away judgmental language you also remove some of the emotional issues that can arise by telling someone that what they are doing is 'wrong'.

Asking Questions

To quote Galileo Gallilei: 'You cannot teach a person anything; you can only help him find it within himself'.

FEEDBACK IN ACTION

Leading on from the example of the bowling practice discussed in the observation and analysis section, I would first take the bowler to one side and ask them what they had noticed about their outcomes – where is the ball going? If they answered that it was inconsistent or going down the leg side I would ask why they thought this was. From there we could begin to discuss the key issue of balance at the crease and find a solution. Depending on the player's awareness, this might be a quick process, or it may involve follow-up questions. But however long it takes, the important thing is that the player is left with a very clear picture of what they need to do to improve.

In this instance one method to help your player may be simply giving them a visual target on top of the stumps to look at when they bowl. When deciding what action to take it is important to communicate clearly with your player and explain why you are suggesting a certain course of action. For example, I would explain to them that the head is a key part of their body when it comes to balance. If they can keep it upright and looking at the target they are more likely to stay balanced at the point of release, which will in turn help them bowl straighter.

The quote from Galileo is around 400 years old, but it is only in relatively recent times that coaching has truly embraced the idea of using questions to develop a player's understanding. In the past coaches tended to 'tell' players what to do rather than allow them the opportunity to come up with the answers themselves. While there is a time and place for getting your message across in a direct way, this can often provide more of a 'quick fix' to a problem than a long-term solution. By encouraging your players to think for themselves you encourage them to become their own coaches and develop as 'thinking cricketers'.

As well as improving their ability to retain new information, this also has an obvious benefit when they step over the white line into a competitive match. Players brought up on a questioning method will be much better equipped to problem solve during a game than those used to being told what to do by their coach.

Although alien to some of us who may have experienced the more old-school approach as players, the concept of questioning is second nature to the youngsters of today.

Their schooling is now built around questioning, and children are encouraged to learn for themselves. Therefore extending this into a cricket environment is perfectly natural for them.

The art of using questioning well is one of the hardest coaching tools to master, but one of the most beneficial. Below are five top tips to help develop your questioning.

What am I trying to find out?

Before speaking to your player(s), think about exactly what it is you are trying to find out. If you are not clear of this at the outset, then your questions may become vague and it can take a long time to get the information that you are looking for. Your questions may focus on technique, how a player is feeling, or you may simply want to check that your players have understood instructions. Whichever of these it is, understanding what you want to find out is crucial in helping shape your questions.

'Open' versus 'closed' questions

Although there may be times when a closed question is useful, open questions are generally much more valuable because the answers you receive will contain more information and will give you more of an insight into the player themselves. For example, instead of asking, 'Do you think that was a good cover drive?' adapt the wording slightly, such as 'What was good about that cover drive?' to encourage a more detailed response. Asking questions that begin with words such as *what*, *why* and *how* will help to ensure they are open.

Try not to let your own answers influence your questions

Although your own opinions are useful in helping you choose what questions to ask, you don't want your thoughts to influence the person you are asking. For example, if a coach asks a player, 'Do you think you would have got out if you had played straight instead of across the line?' the player's answer is likely to be affected by the way the question was asked. In this case they are likely to reply, 'No, they wouldn't have got out if they had played straight', because they think this is what the coach wants to hear. Remember that the answer you are looking for is not necessarily the 'right' answer, it is the player's answer – what *they* believe to be right. If the player is merely led to tell you what you, the coach, already think, then the value of the question is lost.

Listen to the answer

This seems the most obvious advice, but is probably the most overlooked. To be skilled at using questions you also need to be a good listener. The player's answers should drive your next questions and your course of action. It is important to allow players the time to give an answer – and it will take some longer than others. If you jump in too soon you risk preventing what might have been a really valuable response.

It is also important to acknowledge a player's answer and not simply ignore it or cast it aside. There is no such thing as a 'wrong' answer if it is what the player thinks. Some of the most unexpected answers may stimulate the best discussions.

Be specific when asking questions to check for understanding

'Do you understand?!' is probably one of the most over-used and least useful questions you will hear during a coaching session. If you ask a group if they understand something, 99 per cent of the time they will say 'Yes', or grunt something sounding like an agreement. In a group setting, individuals will very rarely admit that they don't understand something for fear of looking stupid; instead they will go with the group consensus and hope to pick it up as they go along. The problem is that if the majority of the group doesn't understand and reacts in the same way, then the message will be lost or the practice will break down.

Thus instead of asking, 'Do you understand?', ask specific questions that will give you proof that the players do indeed know what to do. This could range from 'What is the aim of the practice?' to 'Where do you need to stand?'

COACHING PHILOSOPHY

In an interview with *The Australian* in 2012 Andy Flower said: 'Take every successful coach that has ever been and you will find many different ways of getting your message across. I reckon there is one common thread: every successful coach will have been authentic.'

While there are many values and skills that good coaches have in common – some of which are listed earlier in this chapter – the quote above touches on a very important part of coaching and one that is often neglected in the recreational game: individuality. Every coach who takes the field, whether newly qualified or vastly experienced, has a unique personality and a set of skills and values which are vital in shaping both their own development and that of their players. Whether these are things you have picked up through playing and watching cricket or through other areas of your life, they all form a valuable part of your coaching armory.

I would urge every coach to spend some time thinking about their beliefs, strengths and preferred style as a coach in order to construct their own coaching philosophy. While this is likely to have been influenced by other coaches you have observed – and you should never be ashamed to 'steal' examples of good practice you see in other people – it should be personal to you and should underpin the way you work.

A strong, well thought-out coaching philosophy will help shape the decisions you make, the way you interact with your players and the methods you use. Your approach may well change over time, and that is absolutely fine. This may be based on your success as a coach, your players, the environment you are in and the coaches you work with. And while reviewing and adapting the way you operate is an important part of developing as a coach, don't forget Flower's assertion that the best coaches remain authentic and true to themselves.

CHAPTER 3

PLAYER DEVELOPMENT

If you are already a coach in another sport you may have come across Dr Istvan Balyi's Long Term Athlete Development (LTAD) model. It is an influential five-stage theory that offers guidance on what coaches should do with their players at specific times in their development to help them reach élite level in their sport. It subscribes to the idea that for someone to reach this level they will need to put in around ten years or 10,000 hours of practice – a daunting thought!

Broadly speaking, Balyi recommends that we concentrate on building the athlete first and developing their sport-specific skills later. For the purposes of this book where we are concentrating on players aged around thirteen and under, the first three stages of the LTAD model are worth looking at.

The First Three Stages of the LTAD Model

Stage 1 is the Fundamental Stage and is focused on six- to nine-year-olds. It places huge importance on the development of the physical capabilities and fundamental movements that are used across sports. These incorporate agility, balance, co-ordination and speed – ABCS – and include basic movements such as running, jumping, hopping, striking, throwing. At this age players should be encouraged to play a wide range of sports, and the focus is on fun and enjoyment. In a cricket setting this means introducing basic cricket skills such as striking the ball, and catching and throwing through lots of games, relays and fun activities.

Stage 2 is the Learning to Train Stage which looks at what you should do with players in the next phase of development – ages nine to twelve for boys and eight to eleven for girls. Here, coaches should look to teach players sport-specific technical skills and tactical ideas – it is also called the 'golden age of learning' for sport-specific skills. The focus is on training over competition (70 per cent to 30 per cent), and coaches should avoid encouraging players to specialize in certain roles or positions. This is an important time to work on flexibility, but stamina and strength training should only be done through games, relays and own-body weight activities rather than specialized training. In relation to cricket, this stage is the perfect time to introduce plenty of technical skills. However, you should avoid pigeonholing players as wicketkeepers, opening batsmen and so on, and should give them the opportunity to try many different roles.

Stage 3 is the Training to Train Stage for girls aged eleven to fifteen and boys aged twelve to sixteen. These ages are based around the approximate start and end of the adolescent growth spurt. In this stage the practice competition ratio should be about 60 per cent to 40 per cent, and players should begin to specialize their role. It is also a good time to develop tactics and strategic thinking. Specific fitness development will depend on the player's maturation and growth spurts. In a cricket setting we are starting to get players to specialize their role, and to give them the opportunity to play more matches. There should be a clear competitive focus to practices, and tactical thinking such as field settings and target setting should be promoted.

The ECB's Player Development Model (PDM)

LTAD has been widely adopted across different sports, but the ECB has gone a step further and developed its own cricket-specific development model. The ECB's Player Development Model (PDM) has seven stages, ranging from Early to Élite. As well as looking at what skills, practices and learning are relevant to players in each section, it also looks to identify who those players are, where they play, and what the implications are for the coach.

In this book we will focus mainly on the first two stages of the PDM – Early and Basic. Both stages closely match the LTAD model, albeit from a cricket-specific point of view. It is worth noting that the PDM also allows for the fact that players might be in different stages for different skills. For example, you may have a player in your team who is in the Early stage for bowling but is already in the second stage – Basic – for batting. When identifying your players' needs it is important to take this into account.

Youth cricket is still guilty of dividing players on age alone. Although it can be a useful guideline, try to take in the whole picture and allow players to move between groups based on ability as well as age.

In this book I have tried to cover players from around seven to eight to thirteen years old, ages which cover a significant period of development both physically, mentally and in skill acquisition. The list of suggested skills – by no means exhaustive – is simply meant as a guideline to give you an idea of what a typical mixed-ability group of club players may need at each age. But as with all coaching, there is no substitute for knowing your own players, and you should tailor your 'syllabus' to the needs of your own specific group.

Below is the list of new skills that, typically, will be introduced to a mixed ability age group from under nine to under thirteen. *For each age group please note that as well as introducing new skills you should spend time reinforcing the things learnt previously* – for example U11 players will need to spend time reinforcing the key skills introduced at U9, and so on. You may also want to introduce skills from an older age group if you think your players are ready for them.

Examples of New Skills

Age group: Under nine

Main aim: To give children a fun first taste of cricket, teach them a few basic skills, develop basic athletic movements, and get them enthused about the game.

Method: Small sided games, pair or small group work. Predominantly soft ball.

Key 'new' skills:

Technical:
- Basic grip and overarm bowling action from a standing position
- Batting grip and stance
- Straight drive
- Pull shot
- Run-up and bowl (landing and take-off)
- Close catch
- High catch
- Overarm throw

It is important to allow players to move between groups according to their ability as well as their age.

Tactical:
- Basic rules, for example, how you can get out /how you score runs
- Running between the wickets

Physical and mental:
- ABCS – agility, balance, co-ordination and speed
- Develop confidence through lots of praise and positive reinforcement

Age group: Under eleven

Main aim: To develop existing skills for use in game situations, introduce some tactical understanding, introduce more complex technical skills, reinforce basic movement skills.

Method: Small-sided games, pair and small group work, occasional net. Mix of hard and soft ball.

Key 'new' skills:

Technical:
- Basic spin grips (off and leg)
- Off and on drive
- Back foot drive
- Forward and back defensive – think of a fun, positive way to do this!
- One-hand pick-up and underarmthrow
- Two-hand intercept and crow hop
- Wicketkeeping – stance and basic off and leg take

Tactical:
- Hitting gaps
- Backing up (fielding and batting)
- Bowling areas (line and length)
- Field placings – basic introduction

Physical and mental:
- Reinforce ABCS, introduce flexibility, for example before and after games

- Develop commitment by talking about how to practise effectively
- Start getting players to reflect on their own performance to promote confidence, for example, score themselves out of ten
- Introduce concentration

Age group: Under thirteen

Main aim: To develop existing skills for use in match scenarios, develop tactical understanding – for example, batting game plans, field settings – introduce more complex technical skills, introduce basic mental and fitness drills.

Method: Mixture of nets, match-specific middle practice, team fielding practices, pair and small group work. Nearly all hard ball.

Key 'new' skills:

Technical:
- variation ball, e.g. googly for leg spinner, bowling yorkers for seam bowlers
- Away-swing and in-swing
- Square cut
- Hitting over the top
- Playing spin – using feet and sweep
- Chase and retrieve – individual and with partner
- Wicketkeeping – standing up

Tactical:
- Shot selection
- Batting game plans
- Running singles
- Field settings – attacking and defensive
- Bowling simple variations

Physical and mental:
- Introduce basic strength exercises using your own bodyweight
- Develop concentration through distraction practices, and by giving practices a consequence
- Introduce control of emotions in relation to a game, body language on the field, etc.

PERFECT TECHNICAL MODEL

With its wide-ranging set of complex skills, it is perhaps not surprising that cricket more than most sports has historically been obsessed with the idea of a perfect technical model. But the irony is that the perfect technical model doesn't exist. If you watch a game of cricket at any level – from the playground to the Test arena – you will see any number of different techniques in action. Many of these will be highly successful, but very few, if any, will correspond exactly with what we traditionally think of as the 'text-book' or 'orthodox' method of playing the game.

If you take the England Ashes winning side of 2013 you will see a supremely talented side where all its members did things slightly differently. Alastair Cook, Jonathan Trott, Kevin Pietersen and Ian Bell are among the very best batsmen in the world, but they all bat in a very different way. Even if you were to watch them all play a common shot such as the cover drive, you will notice clear variations in technique. Equally Stuart Broad, James Anderson and Steven Finn have very different bowling actions, but all achieve success.

With that in mind perhaps we should think in terms of a *successful* technical model rather than a *perfect* one. For while we can recognize plenty of differences between players, there are still many similarities. For example, successful batsmen will be still and balanced as the ball is delivered, will move into a stable position, and will look to hit the ball with the full face of the bat.

Top bowlers will have a rhythmical run-up, will ensure their energy and momentum is going towards their target, will have their hips and shoulders aligned at back foot contact, and will keep their head in a position where they can look at their target throughout their action.

These coaching points are common across nearly all successful players no matter what other differences they may have. The ECB has taken this idea a step further by coming up with a series of core principles for batting, bowling, fielding and wicketkeeping. These core principles are not specific to a certain type of shot, but instead relate to more general traits that are important across each discipline.

The coaching points listed in this book are intended to reflect the areas of technique that are shared by the majority. They describe methods that will allow most players to achieve success – but you must never lose sight of the importance of the individual: *if a player is achieving successful and consistent results with a technique that is different to the coaching points, then as long as it won't cause them injury, we should be happy to let them continue in their own unique way.*

If you look at recent stars of world cricket such as record Test wicket-taker Sri Lankan spinner Muttiah Muralitharan or his former teammate, fast bowler Lasith Malinga, both used a technique that you wouldn't find in any kind of coaching manual. However, both have achieved incredible success with their own unique methods.

As a coach, knowledge of the coaching points that good players have in common is an important part of your armoury, but don't be afraid to embrace individuality, too.

CHAPTER 4

WHAT MAKES A GOOD PRACTICE SESSION?

The previous chapters have focused on some of the skills that you, as a coach, need in order to help your players develop. This section will look at what makes a good practice session, and the drills and games you might use.

As discussed in Chapter 1, the practices you choose, how long you spend on each one, and the way you interact with your players, will all depend on the individuals you coach and their specific needs. Remember when planning your session to think about who your players are, and what outcomes you want them to achieve; this will help you come up with the drills best suited to them.

The different permutations to this are endless, but it is important not to make your sessions too complicated. At its simplest, I think there are three main outcomes to a good coaching session, and it is useful to keep these in mind when you are planning and reviewing your practices:

- Is it fun?
- Is it safe?
- Will the players learn something?

If every session you run contains those three simple ingredients, then you won't go far wrong.

Making a Session Fun

As we have already mentioned, one of your most important jobs as a coach is to make sure your players have fun. If they don't enjoy their experience they are unlikely to keep playing cricket in the long term. In the past some coaches might have thought that if players were having a good time, they wouldn't learn anything, but thankfully this outdated notion has long since been cast aside. If your players are enjoying the session they are more likely to be engaged with what you are telling them, and will be motivated to keep improving.

There are many things you can do to help ensure that sessions are enjoyable. Here are four top tips to help make your coaching fun.

Make sure everyone is involved

To run a practice that is enjoyable and effective everyone needs to be involved, and players should have a high number of opportunities to practise the skill in question: if they are not actively involved they will lose interest and become bored. When running your sessions make sure you get your players active quickly, and that they are not kept doing the same thing for too long. For example, if you are running a front foot drive practice with a batsman, wicketkeeper and three fielders, ensure that your players change places every four or five balls, rather than every ten.

Make your practices competitive

Although there have been a few suggestions in recent years that children should not engage in competition, I believe this is nonsense. Sport by its very nature is competitive, and

Make your practices competitive.

more importantly, children thoroughly enjoy it. Instead of debating whether it is a positive thing, think instead of how best to use it in your session. If you are introducing a brand new skill you may not want to bring in competition straight away as it could distract your players from what they are trying to learn. Instead it may be better to use it to test a skill that your players have shown they can perform reasonably consistently. It is also important to note that your practices can involve competitions between teams or a number of players, or an individual versus themselves e.g. setting personal bests.

Praise players and create a positive environment

As mentioned in Chapter 2, praise can be a very powerful tool. As a coach your players look up to you, and giving them positive feedback, whether as individuals or a group, will make them feel good. As outlined earlier, you need to ensure that you don't focus your praise solely on the best players. Success is relative to the individual, and it is important to praise effort as well as achievement.

As a coach you also need to ensure that you are creating a positive environment, where success is celebrated but where it is also absolutely all right to 'fail'. No player is successful all the time, especially when learning new skills, and the only way they will learn is to keep trying. Making sure they know this and aren't afraid to get things wrong is crucial in helping them enjoy their learning.

Introduce something new

If your players are always doing the same thing they will get bored. Adding in new skills and drills each week will help keep them engaged and eager to come to training. As a coach, challenge yourself to make every session unique. Even if you are running a practice you have done many times before, try to think of ways you can adapt it to add in a new challenge. This could be by making the task more difficult, putting the emphasis on a new technique, or by changing the rules to promote a different tactical approach. There are any number of ways to add something novel into your session – the only limit is your imagination!

Making a Session Safe

It goes without saying that safety is paramount to running a good practice session and should underpin everything you do. Safety is not just important for looking after your players' wellbeing, it is crucial to the success of your sessions. Accidents will always happen, but if a preventable incident occurs neither the player nor their parent will be keen on them coming back the following week. Practices that are dangerous are also highly distracting for players, and the quality of their experience will drop if they don't feel safe.

Although you can never 100 per cent guarantee safety, through detailed planning and risk assessments you can help stop many potential incidents before a session even starts. As a coach you should have a risk assessment document for every venue you coach at, and should know what to do in case of an emergency.

If you only coach at one location – such as your local cricket club – then this is fairly straightforward as you only need to have one risk assessment. If you work at multiple venues you will need a risk assessment for each of these. If you are working at a cricket club or sports centre they should have their own risk assessment, so it may be that all you need do is make a copy of it. However, it is still useful to make sure you add in any cricket-specific elements that may be missing.

In addition to this you should check the facility against the risk assessment prior to the start of a session, as the risks may have changed. For example, in an outdoor session the grass may be wet, or indoors there could be a problem with the lighting.

You should also include a section on safety for every session plan that you do, detailing the risks that are specific to that session. You need to consider the following:

- What are the possible risks to my players?
- What can I do to reduce these risks?
- How will I monitor safety during the session?
- What is the emergency procedure?

In addition to these points you need to ensure that you have the contact details for your players' parents, and are aware of any medical conditions they may have. For example if they have asthma you need to know this, and be sure that the player has their inhaler. You also need to know where the first aid kit at your club is, or carry your own with you.

Will the Players Learn Something?

If you are new to coaching it can be hard to know exactly what skills you should be covering with your players. Some techniques are best introduced early in a player's development, while others will not be relevant – or achievable – until they have gained a certain amount of experience and skill.

If you introduce a skill too early and the player can't achieve it, the chances are they will become demotivated. Equally a practice that is too easy for a player, or one they have done many times before, is likely to leave them bored and disengaged.

As you will be working with your players week in, week out, you are best placed to judge where they are currently, and what they need to learn in order to progress. To do this you will need to consider a number of factors, including their age, skill level, experience, their physical development and maturity.

When planning a practice, a good starting point can be to come up with the learning objective, and to ask which part of the game the practice is helping the players improve. This should relate to something that can be specifically applied in a match, such as hitting a front foot drive for four, bowling at the death, taking slip catches. From here you can work back and consider how to plan your practice accordingly – for example what technical, tactical, physical and mental elements should you consider, and what practice type should you use?

Planning Perfect Practices

All coaches crave new practices and drills. None of us wants to miss a trick, and we are always keen for fresh ideas to try out. The great thing is that the list of practices and drills is endless, and the only limit is the coach's imagination.

The practices in this book are some of the ones that have served me well – though don't feel you have to follow them to the letter. Almost all of them have been adapted, tweaked and moulded from practices I have seen delivered by other coaches, or experienced as a player.

The very best coaches are open to the ideas of others, but make them their own, and I would encourage you to do exactly the same with these practices. As a coach you should review and refine your drills as you go. Some may work brilliantly first time, others will need some tweaking; some will go down very well with a certain group, but less well with another. Constantly reflecting on the practices and your own performance is vital in your ongoing development as a coach.

The sections below suggest a few things to consider when planning practices.

Numbers

As coaches I am sure we have all been in a position where we have had to coach a group that we felt was too big. If the group is too large then the quality of the practice can suffer because it is more difficult to give players individual feedback, and managing the behaviour of the group becomes much harder.

The suggested ECB coach-to-player ratio is 1:16 for a normal practice session, and 1:8 for a net session. Some of the practices in this book are designed for smaller groups than this, but the idea is that you can safely run two or three groups doing the same thing at the same time.

Equipment and distances

The equipment and distances set out in the drills below are merely suggestions, and should be adapted as you see fit. The main considerations at all times should be on safety, ensuring that everyone is involved, and making sure the equipment is suitable for your players. For example, you wouldn't use a hard ball with a group of seven-year-olds playing the pull shot for the first time. Neither should your under thirteens be limited to using plastic bats and tennis balls.

In the drills listed, nearly all are suitable for different types of ball, but the majority – particularly the batting practices – have been set out with a soft ball. If you intend to use a hard ball, especially for the batting drills, you will need to increase the distances to ensure that your players remain safe.

For further ideas on adapting practices, please refer to 'differentiation' in Chapter 11.

The ECB continuum of practice

The England and Wales Cricket Board (ECB) has devised a 'practice continuum' to highlight different types of practice. It begins with simple 'fixed practices' at one end, 'variable practices' in the middle, and 'cricket game-based practices' at the other end.

In broad terms it categorizes fixed practices as repetitive drills with few variables – for example, hitting a front-foot drive off a tee. These are typically used when introducing new skills or grooving existing ones. Variable practices require the player to do something different each time – for example, playing a variety of attacking shots to balls that could be thrown on any line or length. These are normally used when trying to go some way to replicate the unpredictable nature of a game. They can be used to increase the challenge or to learn match-specific skills.

A cricket game-based practice gives players the opportunity to practise in 'real-life' match-based scenarios where the demands are random and can cover technical, tactical, physical and mental skills – for example, a conditioned game that replicates the last five overs of a one-day match. These are used to replicate match conditions and to put established skills under pressure.

This book offers practices from across the continuum, with some suggestions of how to make them more fixed or more game-like.

CHAPTER 5

SKILLS, DRILLS AND PRACTICES: WARM-UPS

The idea of a warm-up is simply to prepare your players in body and mind for the training session they are about to take part in. These sessions can take any number of different forms, but for children under the age of thirteen they will typically include some or all of the following: a cricket-related activity or small-sided game, different movement skills, and/or dynamic stretching.

There are many different ways to run a good warm-up, but the key points to remember are that it should:

- be quick and easy for you, as coach, to set up
- be enjoyable
- link into the session you are about to run
- increase in intensity
- incorporate both the body and the mind
- be safe

If you are running a training night of one to two hours, a warm-up should take up no more than a maximum of around ten to fifteen minutes.

Drills and Practices

Hand Hockey
Aim: To develop catching, throwing, teamwork and communication as part of a warm-up.

Equipment: One ball, eight cones.

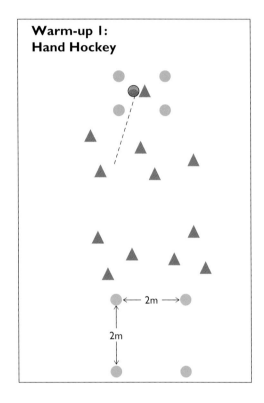

Warm-up 1: Hand Hockey

Number of players: From three to ten per team. Six-a-side is ideal.

Space: For a six-a-side game a netball court-sized space is sufficient, but you can make it work in spaces of varying size.

Explanation: Set up as shown in the diagram, with a scoring zone made up of a $2 \times 2m$ square of cones at each end. Divide the players into two teams and nominate which set of cones each team will score in.

A point is scored if a player catches the ball in their team's designated scoring zone.

To get the ball there teammates must pass underarm to each other. Once they have the ball they cannot run, just as in netball. The team without the ball must try to intercept passes. Once a point is scored, the ball is given to the opposition team and play begins again.

Coaching points: Close catch and high catch technique; underarm throw.

Make it harder: *If a player drops the ball or it bounces before reaching them, possession goes to the other team. *One-handed catching only. *Teams must alternate passes between throwing and rolling the ball along the ground.

Make it easier: *Use a bigger ball. **Make the scoring zones bigger. **Make the pitch smaller.

Batting Relay

Aim: To develop hand–eye coordination, batting grip, and running between wickets as part of a warm-up.

Equipment: One bat, one ball and four cones per group.

Number of players: Teams of up to six.

Explanation: Divide the players into equal teams. In front of each group place two cones about 10–12m apart, with another two equally spaced between them. The first player in each team starts with the bat and ball.

In the first race the player at the front of each team uses the bat like a hockey stick to dribble the tennis ball to the furthest cone

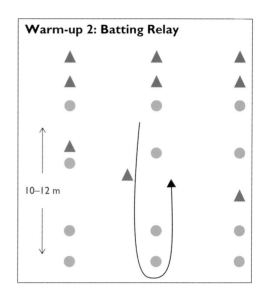

Warm-up 2: Batting Relay

10–12 m

and back. The next player then takes over, like a relay race. The winning side is the first to sit in a line when every player has performed the practice.

The second time through, the players repeat the drill but dribble between the cones.

The third time through they must try and balance the ball on the bat and run to the furthest cone and back – like an egg and spoon race.

The fourth time the players must go to the furthest cone and back while using the bat to bounce the ball up and down.

Finally remove the middle two cones and ball, and each player sprints to the furthest cone and back, in the same way as running a two in a match.

Coaching points:
- Players should use the basic batting grip for all races except the last one.
- When running between wickets players should extend their arm and touch the cone at the far end with the bat, just like reaching for the crease in a match.

Make it harder: *Make players weave between cones for all races. *Bring in more cones to increase dribbling difficulty. *Players must go back to the start if they hit a cone (for the dribbling races), or if they hit the floor (for the balancing/bouncing drills).

Make it easier: *Increase the gap between cones for the weaving race. *Use a bigger ball for races one and two. *Use a tennis racquet instead of a cricket bat for races four and five.

Dynamic Tag

Aim: To prepare the body for activity using dynamic stretches in a fun, competitive game.

Warm-up 3: Dynamic Tag

Equipment: One ball per player, and cones/lines to mark out the playing area.

Number of players: Dependent on space, up to thirty players will fit comfortably into a netball court-sized space.

Explanation: Mark out a rectangular space using cones. Two 'taggers' start with a tennis ball each. Their task is to touch another player with the tennis ball while still holding it. The player they touch is then given a ball and becomes a tagger. The game continues in this way until only one player is left untagged, and they are the winner.

Throughout the game change the way the players move around the area to incorporate different dynamic movements, for example running, skipping, hopping, jumping, heel flicks, high knees, running backwards, side-stepping.

Coaching points: Try to ensure your players are performing each movement efficiently and athletically.

Make it harder (for the taggers): *Make the space bigger. *Make the taggers link arms/hold hands so they must work together. *Make the taggers hold the ball in their weaker hand.

Make it easier (for the taggers): *Give the taggers two balls each. *Players automatically become taggers if they perform the wrong movement – for example run when they should be side-stepping. *Make the space smaller.

Bowling Warm-Up

Aim: To prepare the body for activity in a game that combines bowling and dynamic stretches.

Equipment: One ball and three cones per group.

Number of players: Teams of three to six.

Explanation: Place two cones a pitch length apart, and a third 3–5m behind the one at the bowler's end (see diagram).

Bowlers wait behind cone three. A wicketkeeper should stand behind cone one. The bowler bowls from cone two, the wicketkeeper collects the ball and throws it to the next bowler. The person who bowled the ball replaces the wicketkeeper.

After each bowler has been, change the movements performed while moving between cones, for example side steps, skipping, lunges, high knees, heel flicks, hamstring walks, running backwards.

This should build to a challenge for the last one to two minutes, where the teams are asked to see how many balls they can bowl in that time.

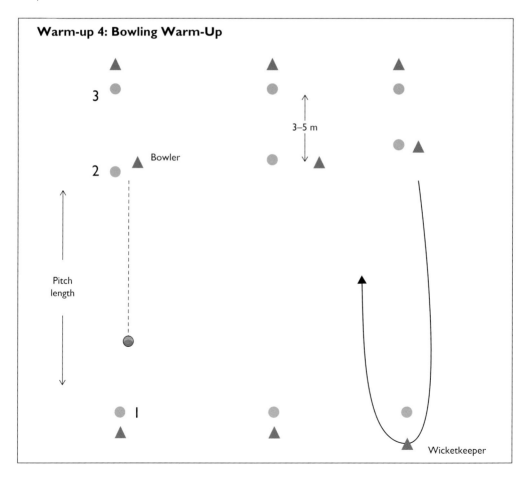

Warm-up 4: Bowling Warm-Up

3

3–5 m

2 Bowler

Pitch
length

1

Wicketkeeper

Coaching points:
- Encourage players to follow through towards the target.
- Try to ensure your players are performing each movement athletically.

Make it harder: *Introduce target zones for the bowlers. *Increase the length of the run-up. *Increase the length of the pitch.

Make it easier: *Players bowl from the base position. *Make the pitch smaller. *Simplify the movements in between stations to running, hopping, jumping and skipping.

Dynamic Stretch Circle Warm-Up

Aim: To prepare the body for activity using dynamic stretches and basic fielding skills.

Equipment: Minimum of one ball and one cone between two. A near limitless number of additional cones, stumps, agility poles, ladders and hurdles can be incorporated.

Number of players: Four to sixteen.

Explanation: Place the cones in a circle about 10m in diameter, an equal distance apart. Place the additional equipment at random in the middle of the circle.

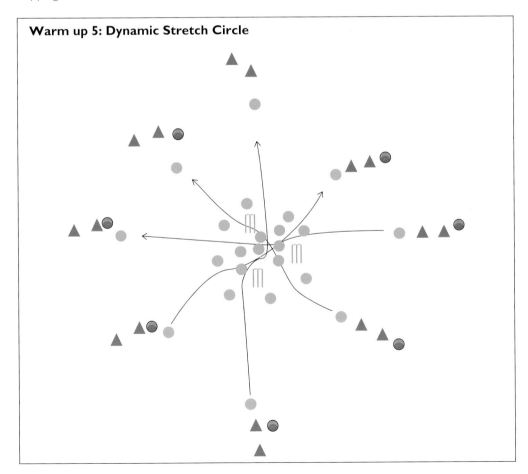

Warm up 5: Dynamic Stretch Circle

Split the group into pairs with one pair on each cone. The first player on each cone starts with the ball.

On your command the first player in each group jogs into the middle and uses fast feet to move in and out of the equipment. When they have negotiated the equipment they throw the ball to a player waiting on the cone opposite, and follow the ball. When the player on the cone receives the ball they repeat the exercise.

As you go along, change the movements performed between cones to include some or all of the following: side steps, skipping, lunges, high knees, heel flicks, hamstring walks, running backwards.

Each player should have the chance to perform each dynamic stretch at least once.

Coaching points: Try to ensure your players are performing each movement athletically, and have their weight on the balls of their feet when moving through the equipment. You can also reinforce the underarm throw and close-catch skills.

Make it harder: *Randomize the cone a player can go to. *Alter the equipment in the middle to include greater agility challenges, for example more ladders or hurdles. *Change the cricket skills to include one-handed catching, one- or two-handed pick-up, or left-handed throwing.

Make it easier: *Remove the equipment from the middle. *Run the drill without a ball so players simply 'high five' each other when they swap places. *Swap dynamic stretches for basic movement skills, for example jogging, hopping, jumping, skipping.

CHAPTER 6

SKILLS, DRILLS AND PRACTICES: BATTING

Coaching Batting

To win a cricket match you need to score more runs than the other team. That is the straightforward bit. But in a game where you get just one chance and everything – from the eleven opposing players to the weather – can contribute to your downfall, it is a far from simple discipline.

As a coach you need to focus not just on a batsman's technical skills but also on their ability to adapt to different playing conditions, game situations and types of bowler. A good batsman needs to be comfortable on the front and back foot, confident against seam and spin bowling, and must be able to think on their feet. And above all else they need to be able to score runs!

Traditionally coaches would get players to concentrate on 'not getting out' rather than scoring runs. For example, I am sure that for many people reading this book the first shot they learned was the forward defensive shot. But not only is this a dull and uninspiring introduction to cricket, it actively hinders the creation of the sort of dynamic, attack-minded players that the modern game requires. Young players (and older ones!) love to hit the ball hard, and this should be encouraged throughout your coaching.

Of course a solid defence is still important, but as coaches we should be creative in the way we introduce it and think about how to make the front and back foot defensive shots positive options rather than negative ones.

If you watch any game of cricket you will notice that top batsmen will have their own personal style. However, there are a number of key skills they all share.

The practices that follow are designed to help you provide your young players with some of the building blocks that will support them in becoming adaptable, fast-thinking run scorers.

The Basics

Grip
When picking up the bat the batsman should have both hands together in the middle of the handle. For right-handed players the right hand should be at the bottom and the left hand on top; for left handers it would be the

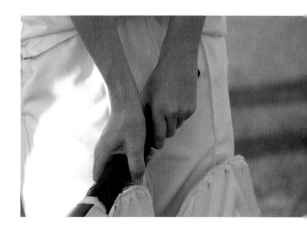

Batting grip.

reverse. The thumb and index finger form a 'V' shape, and the 'V' on each hand should be in line one with the other, half way between the splice of the bat and the outside edge.

In order to be in full control of the bat, the player should grip it tightly with their top hand and more loosely with their bottom hand.

Stance

When waiting to face the ball a batsman needs to be in a balanced and comfortable position. It is particularly important that the head is still and the eyes level at the point when the bowler lets go of the ball.

The batsman should stand side-on to the bowler with their feet in line with each other and parallel to the crease; how far apart they are will depend on the player's height and personal preference. In young players a good starting point is for them to be around a shoulder's width apart. Whatever position the player chooses, their stance should allow them to move forwards or back quickly as required.

When waiting for the ball most players like to pick up their bat. If this is the case they should bring it back in a straight line and hold it around waist height. A good guide for young players is that their top hand should be level with their back hip – thus for right-handers their left hand should be level with their right hip.

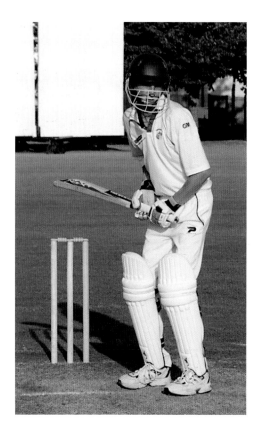

Batting stance – front view.

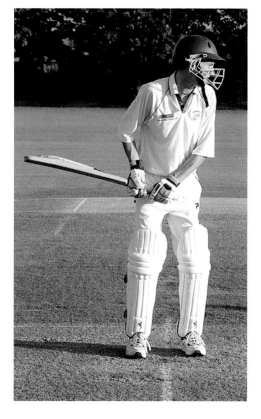

Batting stance – side view.

PRE-DELIVERY MOVEMENTS

If you watch professional cricket you may see a number of players making a small movement with their feet just before the bowler releases the ball. These pre-delivery or trigger movements are designed to help the batsman feel balanced and prepared for the ball. Typically they involve a 'forward press' – a half step forwards with the front leg, or a shuffle back and across towards the off side. When executed well they can give a batsman a sense of rhythm and extra time to play the ball.

Many youngsters watch these movements on television and try to replicate them without understanding why. In most cases this will have a negative effect, leaving them off balance and rushed, often limiting their potential scoring areas. For young players the best advice remains to stay as still as possible at the crease. As they get older this may change, but I have rarely – if ever – seen a young player under thirteen improved by a trigger movement.

Backswing and step

When lifting the bat to play a shot the batsman should take it back in a straight line. In order to generate power the bat should be slightly higher than the stumps. The timing of this movement should coincide with the batsman moving their feet forward or back depending on the shot they are playing. To ensure a smooth, powerful swing players should lift their bat with their arms rather than their hands.

Feeding for Batting

Feeds are vital to determining the success of any drill but are particularly important in a batting practice: if the ball is not thrown on the right line and length then the batsman won't be able to perform the required skill effectively. For example, if they are practising the pull shot and the ball is too full, they will end up trying to pull a ball they shouldn't or playing a completely different shot.

The type of feed you use will depend on the ability of the player, the ball you use, the surface you are playing on, and the drill itself. Below is a list of the type of feeds you may use and when you might use them.

Hitting off a tee

Batting tees can be bought from all good cricket suppliers and are a vital part of a coach's kitbag. They are great to use when you are teaching young players new shots as

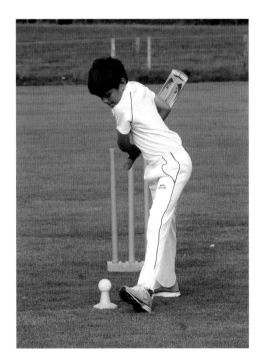

Hitting off a tee – a great way to help beginners to hit the ball cleanly.

the ball is stationary so it will be in the right place for them to hit every time. This allows the player to concentrate on the technique itself, and means they will achieve a high level of success.

For front foot drive practices place the tee a comfortable stride (the player's) from the batsman's starting position, and adjust the line as appropriate to focus on the straight, cover or drives.

If you are working on a back foot shot – for example the pull or cut – then you can still use a tee: all you need do is place it on top of a stump. It is preferable to use plastic stumps for this as players will often make contact with the ball, tee and stump at the same time; if you were to use wooden stumps this could cause damage to the player, their bat and the stumps themselves.

Drop feeds

If your players are achieving a consistently high level of success hitting off a tee, the next step for front foot drives is to get them striking the ball from a drop feed. As the name suggests, a drop feed is when the ball is simply dropped on to the right line and length, and the player hits it after it has bounced. This is still fairly simple because there is little variation in the feed, but the player does have to judge the bounce of the ball.

A drop feed can be performed by the batsman themselves or by a partner. If it is the latter, make sure they drop the ball at arm's length and stand in a position where they will not be hit by the bat – usually this will be to the off side of the batter.

If you are using this type of feed make sure that you have the right type of ball and

The drop feed – the next level of challenge up from a tee.

The drop feed (continued).

surface. If the ball doesn't bounce or the surface is uneven then the skill cannot be performed correctly. Generally if you are using a tennis ball on a hard surface – for example a sports hall floor – then the batsman should let the ball bounce two or three times before striking it to ensure they are hitting in the middle of the bat. Simply change the line the ball is dropped on to practise the straight, cover and on drives.

Full toss feeds

If you are working on back foot shots, then using a drop feed is problematic as it won't bounce high enough. Instead try using a full toss feed thrown underarm from the point where the ball would have bounced. For example if you are working on the pull shot, the feeder should throw from around 3–4m away. Ideally the feeder should be kneeling to replicate the way a ball rises after bouncing.

With this type of feed you also need to consider the height and speed of the ball. These variables will both depend on the player you are working with. Beginners will need a fairly slow feed to give them time to get into position, whilst more experienced batsmen can cope with a quicker ball. How high the ball needs to be will depend on the player's own height. For the back foot defence, pull and cut shots waist height is a good guide, while for the back foot drive the ideal height is half way between knee and waist.

Bobble feeds

Although you can use full toss feeds for front foot drives, a better option is the bobble feed. This is the natural progression from the drop feed, and like that option, you will need to consider the type of ball and surface you use.

The feeder should be positioned around 5m from the batter. They throw the ball underarm, attempting to get it to bounce

The bobble feed.

The bobble feed (continued).

several times before it reaches the batsman. The idea of this feed is that the ball should arrive as a half volley, and will therefore always be the right length to drive. As with previous feeds you can simply adjust the line to work on different drives.

Overarm feed

The next step on from the feeds described above is to use an overarm feed. Depending on how high you want the ball to bounce, this can be done from a standing position or from a feeder on one knee. How far back they stand and how hard they throw will depend on the shot, the ability of the player, and the ball/equipment you are using. Unless you are purposely trying to limit a batsman's reaction time you should ensure the feeder is far enough back so that the batsman has time to get into position without being rushed.

To help improve the accuracy of feeds it can be useful to give the feeder a target to aim at. This could be a square marked with cones or a line on a sports hall floor.

Finally on feeding

Sometimes it is possible for you to do all the feeding in one session, but more often than not you will need your players to feed the ball to each other to ensure that everyone is actively involved. To help them feed accurately and to develop their own skills, make sure that when they feed they use proper cricket techniques. For example, if they are bobble feeding make sure they use the underarm throw, if overarm make sure they practise their throwing technique. Too often I have seen players end up feeding with a sort of darts technique which they think will help them be more accurate. Not only is the opposite true, but it also hinders the development of their own skills.

Batting Practices

Front Foot Drive

Description: The front foot drive is an attacking shot played to a full length delivery known as a half-volley.

There are three types of front foot drive: the straight drive, the off drive (also called the 'cover' drive) and the on drive. These shots are named after the area of the field the player is hitting the ball to. All are played to a ball a little fuller than one you might defend. Which drive the batsman plays will depend on the line of the ball – for example, outside off stump for a cover drive, on off or middle stump for a straight drive, and on middle and leg for the on drive.

Match-based objective: To hit a full length ball powerfully along the ground for four using the front foot drive.

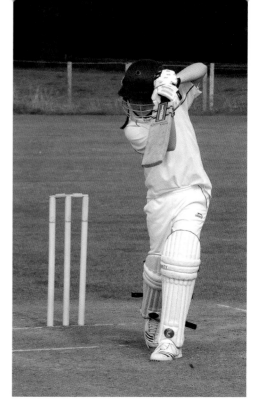

Front foot drive – the player should look to hit the ball with the full face of the bat and remain balanced throughout.

Practice Drill for Front Foot Drive

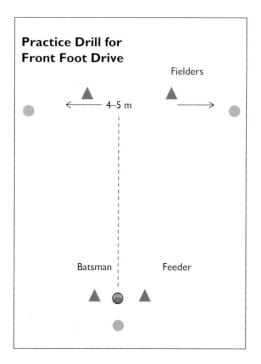

Fielders

←—— 4–5 m ——→

Batsman

Feeder

Coaching points:

- The batsman should move their leading shoulder and head towards the ball.
- The front foot should follow, taking a big stride towards the ball to create a stable base.
- Players should look to hit powerfully using the full face of the bat.
- The batsman's head should be over the ball at the point of contact, with their front knee bent.
- After contact the player should follow through, bringing their bat over, or level with, their leading shoulder.
- They should remain balanced throughout the shot.

Top tip: Encourage your players to maintain a loose grip on the bat with their bottom hand. It should feel as though it is almost being held by the thumb and index finger alone.

Practice drill for front foot drive

Aim: To get players hitting a powerful front foot drive.

Equipment: One bat, one ball and two cones.

Number of players: Four to six per group.

Explanation: Set up a 'goal' 4–5m wide and about 8–10m from the batsman, using cones. Two players stand in the goal acting as fielders, one player is the feeder and the fourth is the batter. If you have more players you can add more fielders or include a wicketkeeper.

The feeder should drop the ball at arm's length so it bounces a comfortable step from the batsman. The batter hits it on the second or third bounce using the front foot drive, and attempts to strike it powerfully along the ground and through the goal. The fielders try and stop the ball and return it to the feeder. The batsman scores one point if they hit the ball in line with the goal and the fielder stops it, or four points if it goes through the goal. Each player should have four goes, then change position moving clockwise.

This same practice will also work for the off and on drives by simply moving the goal to different positions. For the off drive, move the goal in line with cover; for the on drive, place a goal between mid-on and mid-wicket.

Make it harder: *Use a bobble or overarm feed. *Make the goal smaller. *Add extra goals at cover and mid-wicket so the player has to choose where to hit the ball.

Make it easier: *Hit off a tee. *Make the goal bigger. *Remove scoring so players just focus on the skill.

Pull Shot

Description: The pull shot is an attacking shot played to a short ball pitching anywhere from just outside off stump to just outside leg stump. It is played with a horizontal bat and the ball is hit on the leg side, typically between fine leg and mid wicket.

Match-based objective: To hit a short ball for four, pull shot powerfully down and for four through the leg side.

Coaching points:
- The back foot should move back and across towards the off side, staying parallel to the crease to allow the player to get their head in line with the ball.
- Players should take a big backswing, getting their hands above the ball.
- The player should move their front foot back and towards the leg side so they are chest on to the ball.
- Keeping the head still, the player should hit the ball powerfully down and into the leg side using a horizontal bat and with their arms fully extended.
- The bat should continue up and over the batsman's front shoulder.
- They should finish in a balanced position.

Top tip: Help your player stay balanced by encouraging them to keep looking at where the ball was even after they have hit it.

Practice drill for pull shot

Aim: To hit a pull shot with power and control.

Equipment: One ball, one set of stumps, one bat and two cones per group.

Number of players: Five to six per group.

Pull shot – notice how the player moves his feet to turn his chest to the ball.

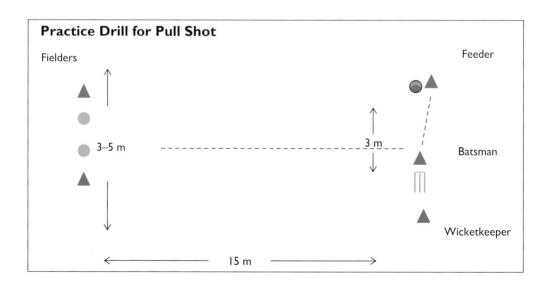

Practice Drill for Pull Shot

Fielders

Feeder

3–5 m

3 m

Batsman

Wicketkeeper

15 m

Explanation: Set up a goal 3–5m wide between square leg and mid-wicket, about 15m from the batter. Position two fielders in the goal, a wicketkeeper behind the stumps, and a feeder kneeling 3m from the batsman. The feeder throws the ball underarm, aiming to get it to the batter at waist height. The batsman uses a pull shot to try and hit the ball through the goal. They score one point if the fielders stop the ball in line with the goal, and four for scoring a 'goal'. Each batter has four goes, then the players change places, moving in a clockwise direction.

Make it harder: *Use an overarm bouncing feed. *Make the goal smaller or further away. *Only award the player points if the ball bounces before reaching the goal.

Make it easier: *Hit from a tee positioned on a stump. *Allow the batsman to hit from a chest-on position as though they have already moved their feet. *Make the goal bigger.

Back foot drive

Description: The back foot drive is an attacking shot played to a ball that is slightly fuller than one you would typically pull, but too short to play off the front foot.

Like the front foot drive, it is played with a straight bat and can be hit on the off side, leg side or straight depending on the line of the ball.

Match-based objective: To use the back foot drive to hit a ball that is short of a length along the ground through cover, mid-wicket or straight for two or four.

Coaching points:
- The back foot should move back and across towards the off side, staying parallel to the crease, to allow the player to get their head in line with the ball.

Back foot drive – note how the batsman goes up onto his toes to get over the ball.

- The front foot should follow, moving next to the back foot.
- Players should look to hit powerfully using the full face of the bat.
- The batsman's head should be over the ball at the point of contact, with their weight on their back leg.
- After contact, the player should follow through bringing their hands level with their eyes.
- They should remain balanced throughout the shot.

Top tip: Encourage your players to move into position quickly and use the full depth of their crease. This will give them more time and help them control the shot.

Practice drill for back foot drive
Aim: To play a controlled back foot drive.

Equipment: One bat, one ball, one set of stumps and two cones per group.

Number of players: Five or six.

Explanation: Using two cones, set up a 'goal' 11m away and about 3–4m in width. It should be in line with the cover position, for example 60 degrees from the batter on the off side. Start with two fielders in the goal, a wicketkeeper behind the stumps, and a feeder around 3m in front of the batter. The feeder throws the ball underarm in line with off stump, between knee and waist high. The batter should play a back foot drive, looking to hit the ball back through the goal.

They score one point if the fielders stop the ball in line with the goal, and four for scoring a 'goal'. Each batter has four goes, and then the players change places, moving in a clockwise direction.

The same practice will also work for the other types of back foot drive – simply move the goal straight or between mid-wicket and mid-on.

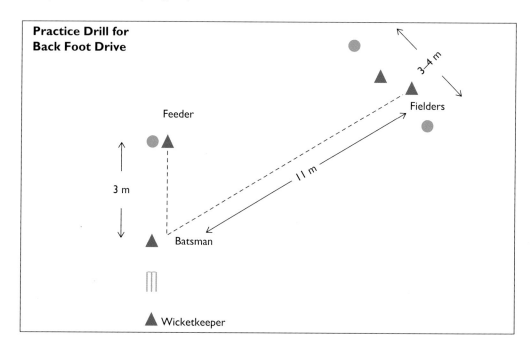

Practice Drill for Back Foot Drive

3–4 m

Feeder

Fielders

11 m

3 m

Batsman

Wicketkeeper

Front foot defence.

Make it harder: *Use an overarm bounce feed. *Make the goal smaller. *Add goals straight and at mid-wicket so the player has to choose where to hit the ball.

Make it easier: *Make the goal bigger. *Position the feeder further away so the player has more time to react. *Allow the batsman to move into position before the ball is thrown.

Front Foot Defence

Description: The front foot defence is a defensive shot played to a good length ball that would go on to hit the stumps. A good length means it is too short to drive, but not short enough to play on the back foot.

Match-based objective: Players should use the front foot defence to stop a full length ball hitting the stumps, using the full face of the bat and keeping the ball down.

Coaching points:
- The batsman should move their leading shoulder and head towards the ball.
- The front foot should follow, taking a big stride towards the ball to create a stable base.
- Players should look to make contact with the face of the bat angled down.
- The batsman's head should be over the ball at the point of contact, with their front knee bent.
- They should remain balanced throughout the shot.

Top tip: Encourage players to wait for the ball to hit the bat and play with 'soft hands'. This means relaxing their grip on the bat to allow the ball to drop to the ground quickly.

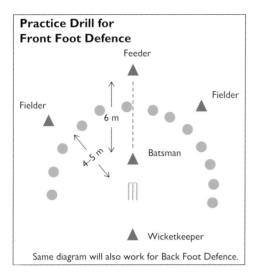

Practice Drill for Front Foot Defence

Feeder

Fielder

6 m

4-5 m

Batsman

Fielder

Wicketkeeper

Same diagram will also work for Back Foot Defence.

Practice drill for front foot and back foot defence

Aim: To play a solid front foot defence with soft hands.

Equipment: One bat, one ball, one set of stumps and eight cones per group.

Number of players: Three to seven.

Explanation: Set up with a batter in front of a set of stumps, a wicketkeeper behind them, and a feeder around 6m away. You also need to set up a half circle of cones about 4–5m in front the batter – if you have fielders they should stand outside the cones.

The feeder should throw a tennis ball under-arm so that it bounces about 1–1.5m in front of the batter. The batsman plays a forward defence and attempts to make the ball bounce inside the ring of cones. They get a point for every time they manage this. Each batter has four goes and then the players change places, moving in a clockwise direction.

Make it harder: *Use an overarm bounce feed. *Make the ring of cones smaller. *Place fielders 3m from the bat – the batter must now avoid being caught out.

Make it easier: *Use a bobble feed. *Make the cone zone bigger. *Use a less bouncy ball, for example a low compression tennis ball.

Back Foot Defence

Description: The back foot defence is a defensive shot that can be played to any length from just back of a good length to a short-pitched delivery. It is played with a straight bat, and the main purpose is to defend your stumps and stop the ball going in the air.

Match-based objective: To use the back foot defence to defend a short ball using the full face of the bat and keeping the ball down.

Coaching points:
- The back foot should move back and across towards the off side, remaining parallel to the crease, to allow the player to get their head in line with the ball.

Note how the bat remains straight with the head over the ball to keep it down.

- The front foot should follow, moving next to the back foot.
- The batsman's head should be over the ball at the point of contact, with their weight on their back leg.
- The bat should be vertical, with the face angled down towards the ground.
- The batter should remain balanced throughout the shot.

Top tip: Encourage your players to use the full depth of their crease and to move towards the off side. You can encourage this by placing a cone to the leg side of their back foot. If they go to the leg side they will step on it and become more aware of their movements.

Practice drill for back foot defence
Aim: To play a solid back foot defence with soft hands.

Equipment: One bat, one ball and a set of stumps per group.

Number of players: Five to nine.

Explanation: Set up with a batsman in front of the stumps, a wicketkeeper behind them, and a feeder about 6m away. You will also need at least one fielder on each side at least 4m from the bat.

The bowler feeds the ball overarm from a kneeling position so it lands about half way between themselves and the batter, and bounces at about waist height.

Using only a back foot defence shot or a leave, the batsman tries to avoid being bowled or caught by a fielder. The feeder and fielders rotate every six balls, but the batsman stays in until they are out. The winning batsman is the one who faces the most balls before they are out.

Make it harder: *Use an overarm bounce feed from a standing position. *Add more fielders. *Introduce a 'one hand, one bounce' rule so the batsman can be out if the fielder catches the ball one-handed after it has bounced.

Make it easier: *Move the fielders further back, or replace with cones as in the front foot defence practice. *Remove the stumps so they can only be caught out. *Use an underarm full toss thrown from closer to the batsman.

The Square Cut
Description: The square cut is an attacking shot that is played to a short-pitched ball outside off stump. It is played using a horizontal bat, and as its name suggests, it is hit square of the wicket on the off side.

Square cut 1.

Square cut 2.

Match-based objective: To use the square cut to hit a short ball outside off stump powerfully down and for four square on the off side.

Coaching points:
- The back foot should move back and across towards the line of the ball, staying parallel to the crease.
- The batsman should take a powerful back-swing ensuring their hands are higher than the ball.
- Their head should be over the ball at the point of contact, with their weight on their back leg.
- They should strike the ball powerfully with a horizontal bat, looking to hit the ball down and through the cover point area.

- They should remain balanced throughout the shot and follow through with their bat up over their front shoulder.

Top tip: Start players off hitting from the top of the backswing after they have already moved their back foot into position. This will help them feel what it is like to hit from a stable base.

Practice drill to play a square cut
Aim: To play a powerful and controlled square cut.

Equipment: One bat, one ball, two cones and a set of stumps per group.

Number of players: Five or six.

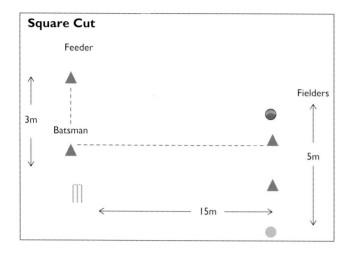

Square Cut

Feeder

Fielders

3m

Batsman

5m

15m

Playing Spin – Moving Out of the Crease to Drive

Description: Moving out of the crease to drive is a method usually employed against spin bowlers to negate the threat they pose and create scoring opportunities. It involves the batsman advancing down the wicket towards the bowler rather than waiting for the ball to reach them. This can be a useful tactic as it means the batsman can reach the ball before it has had a chance to spin. It also puts the bowler off their line and length.

Explanation: Set up with a batsman in front of the stumps, a wicketkeeper behind them, and a feeder about 3m from the batsman. Place two cones 3–5m apart between backward point and cover, about 15m from the batsman.

The bowler feeds the ball underarm from a kneeling position, aiming to get it about a bat's length outside off stump and around waist high. The batsman uses the square cut to try and hit the ball through the goal. They score one point if the fielders stop the ball in line with the goal, and four for scoring a 'goal'. Each batsman has four goes, and then the players change places, moving in a clockwise direction.

Make it harder: *Use an overarm bounce feed. *Make the goal smaller. *Take points off if the ball is caught or doesn't bounce before reaching the goal.

Make it easier: *Hit off a tee (placed on a stump). *Allow the player to move their feet prior to the feed so they are already in position to hit. *Make the goal bigger.

Match-based objective: Players should be able to move out of the crease to spinners in a balanced position that allows them to play the front foot drive or the front foot defensive shot as required.

Coaching points:
- Remaining side-on to the bowler and with the weight on the balls of the feet, the player should advance down the wicket ensuring their body stays slightly to the off-side of the ball.
- This movement can be made in one of two ways:
  (i) Using small steps the batsman can bring their back foot in front of their front foot and then step forwards with their front foot; this should be repeated as many times as is needed to get into position to hit the ball.
  (ii) Using small steps the batsman should advance down the wicket in a side-stepping motion, for example moving their front foot forwards and bringing the back foot to join it.

- As they reach the ball they should be in a balanced position as for the front foot drive (see above).

Top tip: When players are moving out to drive, get them to imagine there is a magnet pulling their front shoulder and head so these are the parts of the body that lead the way.

Practice drill for playing spin
Aim: To advance down the wicket in a quick and balanced way and hit a front foot drive.

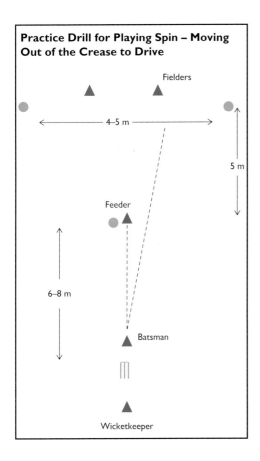

Practice Drill for Playing Spin – Moving Out of the Crease to Drive

Fielders

4–5 m

5 m

Feeder

6–8 m

Batsman

Wicketkeeper

Equipment: One bat, one ball, two cones and a set of stumps per group.

Number of players: Five or six.

Explanation: Set up with a batsman in front of the stumps, a wicketkeeper behind them, and a feeder about 6–8m away. Place a 4–5m wide 'goal' made from cones about 5m behind the feeder, and place two fielders in the goal. The feeder throws a bobble feed to the batter, who comes down the wicket and strikes it through the goal using a front foot drive. Each batter has four goes and then the players change places, moving in a clockwise direction. You can award points as for the front foot drive practice.

Make it harder: *Use an overarm feed. *Add goals at cover and mid-wicket, and nominate where the batsman should hit. *Get the feeder to put spin on the ball. *Get the batsman to hit over the fielders.

Make it easier: *Use a tee or drop feed 3m from the batter so they can practise footwork against a ball that isn't moving towards them. *Make the goal bigger. *Use a bigger ball, for example a mini football.

Quick Singles
Description: As well as teaching players the core technical skills they need, it is also important to introduce them to fundamental tactical approaches. One of these is running quick singles.

Obviously there are many different ways to score a single, but in this instance we are looking to encourage players to score from a ball they would otherwise just defend. By using soft hands to drop the ball close to the wicket, players can keep the scoreboard ticking over and rotate the strike even in the face of good bowling.

HITTING OVER THE TOP

The lofted drive is a shot that often goes hand in hand with moving out of the crease to attack bowlers. It is an aggressive shot used to try and score boundaries and make the opposing captain put fielders out in the deep. This in turn can make it easier to score runs, as there are more gaps in the ring.

The technique for the lofted drive is the same as the front foot drive, but with a few subtle differences. Players should look to hit the ball slightly earlier than on the conventional drive, and their bodyweight should be just behind the point of contact.

To practise hitting over the top, use the 'playing spin' practice, but move the fielders slightly further back. Batsmen should be awarded four points if they score a goal, and six if they hit it over the fielders.

Match-based objective: To play with soft hands to drop the ball down near to the wicket, or deflect it into a gap for a quick single.

Coaching points: If the ball is full, the main coaching points are the same as for the front foot defence. If it is short, the coaching points are the same as for the back foot defence.

- The batsman should allow the ball to hit the bat rather than pushing hard at it.
- The hands should be relaxed ('soft hands') to cushion the ball as it hits the bat.
- After playing the shot, players should be on the balls of their feet, looking for a run.

Top tip: Soft hands can be practised in a number of different ways. These include 'giving' with the hands when catching, and controlling the ball on a tennis racquet. To practise this, the player throws a tennis ball in the air and attempts to stop it dead on the face of the racquet without it falling off.

Practice game for quick singles
Aim: To use soft hands to run quick singles.

Equipment: Two bats, one ball, ten cones and two sets of stumps per group.

Number of players: Twelve for a normal practice, twenty if running as a team game.

Explanation: Set up a normal length pitch with stumps and a batsman at each end. Place a 25m circle of cones around the pitch. A feeder (possibly the coach) should stand about two-thirds of the pitch length from the batsman, who is on strike. All fielders must be outside the circle of cones until the ball is released by the feeder, who throws the ball overarm to the batsman.

The aim for the batsmen is to score as many runs as possible as a pair. There are no boundaries, and they can only score runs if the ball remains inside the circle of cones. They can be out in all the usual ways, and they lose five runs each time one of them is dismissed. Each pair bats for twelve balls: six of these should be full length and six short, so they practise playing off both the front and the back foot.

Make it harder: *Make the circle smaller. *Vary the feed at random. *Introduce bowlers and play like a game of pairs cricket but with the restrictions still in place.

Make it easier: *Use an underarm or bobble feed. *Make the circle bigger. *Limit feed to either the front or the back foot.

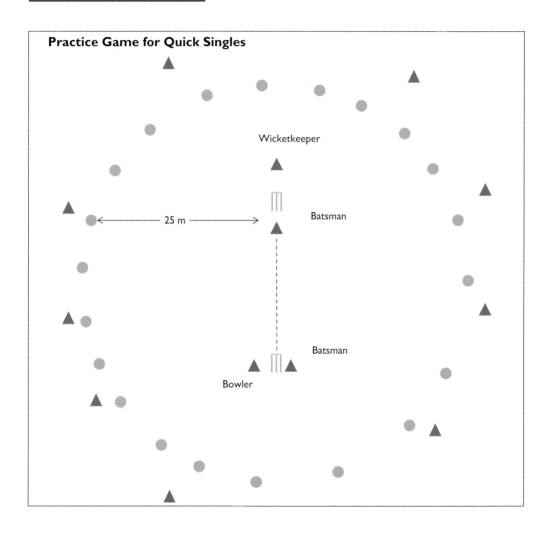

Practice Game for Quick Singles

Wicketkeeper

25 m

Batsman

Batsman

Bowler

Hitting Gaps

Description: There are few more frustrating things as a coach than seeing your player hit a beautiful shot straight to a fielder. From an early age we should encourage our players to look for gaps and hit the ball into areas of the field where there are no fielders. This increases the chances of scoring runs, and also forces the opposition to change their field-setting and/or bowling plans.

Match-based objective: Players should be able to identify where gaps are in the field, and attempt to hit the ball there.

Coaching points: Simple things that may help players hit gaps include playing the ball slightly later, opening or closing the bat face, and using soft hands. The core technical skills of establishing a balanced base, and keeping the head still and the eyes level at the point of contact, are still important.

Top tip: It may be hard as coach to work out whether a player is not seeing the gaps, or is finding it hard to adjust their technique to hit the ball into them. Use questioning throughout the session to find out what players are seeing and what they are trying to do.

Practice game for hitting gaps
Aim: To maximize run scoring by hitting the ball into gaps.

Equipment: Two bats, one ball, twenty-four cones and two sets of stumps per group.

Number of players: Twelve for a normal practice, twenty if running as a team game.

Explanation: Set up the pitch as in the quick singles practice, but instead of the circle of cones, create six 5 × 5m boxes from cones, positioned at least 12m from the batsmen

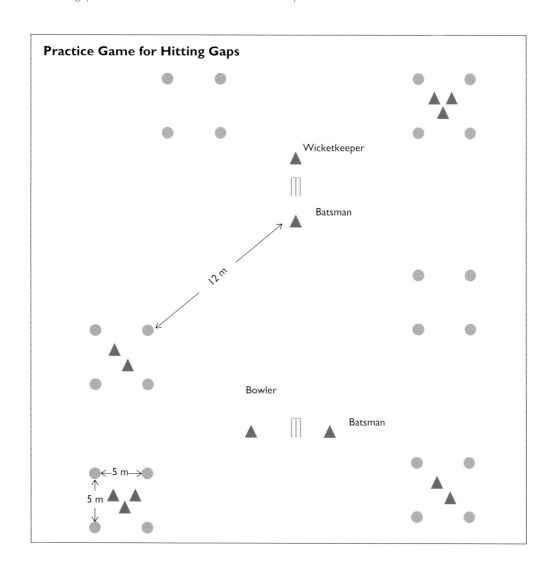

Practice Game for Hitting Gaps

Wicketkeeper

Batsman

12 m

Bowler

Batsman

5 m

5 m

at various places in the outfield. Where you place them is up to you, but a good starting point is roughly at third man, fine leg, cover, mid-wicket, mid-off and mid-on.

As coach you decide how many fielders to place in each box: you can place them all in one box or distribute them evenly, but you need to make sure there is at least one obvious gap for the batsmen to hit into. You can change this at any time. The fielders must remain in their box until the ball has been released by the feeder.

The aim for the batsmen is to score as many runs as possible as a pair. You can have boundaries or make them run everything. They can be out in all the usual ways, and they lose five runs each time one of them is dismissed. Each pair bats for twelve balls. The feeds should be overarm, pitching on a good length, but can vary depending on which gap you want to encourage the batsmen to hit into – for example, shorter feeds if the gaps are square of the wicket.

Make it harder: *Have fewer gaps, or make the boxes bigger (and therefore the gaps smaller). *Vary the feed at random. *Introduce bowlers and play like a game of pairs cricket but with the restrictions still in place.

Make it easier: *Use a bobble or underarm feed. *Make the gaps bigger, or have more of them. *Take away the threat of players being out bowled or caught so they have more freedom to experiment with shots.

Front Foot Drive: Mental and Physical Practice

Description: To help produce a well rounded cricketer we need to make sure that we develop a player's mental and physical attributes as well as their technical and tactical skills. Although these may be areas you focus on in more detail as players get older, there

are a number of simple ways to introduce mental and physical factors into a practice.

Physical skills to develop include speed, strength, power, flexibility, endurance and agility. Mental skills include concentration, commitment, confidence and control. The drill below incorporates a number of these different attributes.

Match-based objective: To use the front foot drive to score runs while under a number of the mental and physical pressures you might find in a match.

Coaching points: When coaching any physical or mental attribute, keep observing the cricket skill and ensure that the standard of this is maintained throughout the practice.

Top tip: When working with young players make sure that any physical drills are appropriate for the player. For players under the age of thirteen physical factors should be introduced to test their ability to perform a skill rather than to specifically improve and develop it – that comes later.

Practice drill for front foot drive
Aim: To develop physical and mental skills during a front foot drive practice.

Equipment: One bat, six red balls and six yellow (different colours and quantities are fine), two red cones and two yellow (the colour of the balls must correspond with the cones).

Number of players: Four to six per group.

Explanation: Set up with two goals – one red, one yellow – 4–5m wide and about 8–10m from the batsman using cones. One should be at mid-off, the other at mid-on. Place a fielder

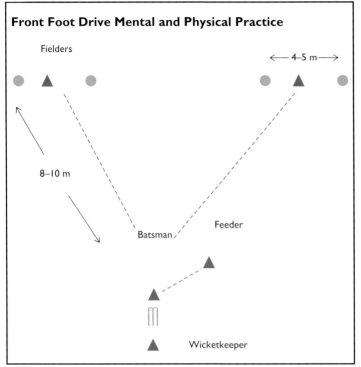

Front Foot Drive Mental and Physical Practice

Fielders

← 4–5 m →

8–10 m

Batsman

Feeder

Wicketkeeper

- To begin with the batsman can choose which goal to hit through.
- Next time round they must hit the first six through the off-side goal and six through the leg-side goal.
- The feeder nominates which goal they hit through by calling either yellow or red as they drop it.
- The feeder nominates red balls to be hit with a full follow-through, and yellow with a checked follow-through – the previous point still applies.
- The batter must hit on the first bounce and the feeder increases the repetition of the feeds.

in each goal (or more, depending on the size of group).

The feeder should drop the ball at arm's length so it bounces one comfortable step from the batsman. The batsman hits it on the second or third bounce using the front foot drive, and attempts to strike it powerfully along the ground and through one of the goals. The fielders try and stop the ball and return it to the feeder. Each player has twelve goes each before changing places.

From this starting point the exercise can be built up to work a number of different technical, tactical, mental and physical skills. The following is a list of progressions:

- Change the command so the player must now hit red balls through the yellow cones and yellow balls through the red.
- If the player misses their intended target or hits to the wrong goal they have to sprint half-way up the pitch and back.

Make it harder/ make it easier: You can vary the feeds and the size of goal as required, but the list of progressions above should also give you some guidance. Some players will be able to work their way through all of them, while others will only manage one or two.

INTRODUCING A HARD BALL

When planning your practices it is important to think about the type of ball you use. Cricket is played with a hard ball, but there are times – particularly when coaching children – when this may not be the best option. Therefore before introducing a hard ball you need to make sure that your players have sufficient technical skill (and protective equipment if batting) to use one safely. If you use it too soon, players will become scared, which will affect both their enjoyment and their ability to perform the skill.

A good way to introduce a hard ball is to begin using it for simple fielding practices and warm-ups where there is little risk of injury. As players become more confident you can start using it in more practices and in small-sided games.

When choosing which ball to use, also take into account the type of practice you are doing, the space you have, and the surface you are playing on. In certain situations tennis balls, windballs or incrediballs are better than cricket balls, even if you are working with older groups.

CHAPTER 7

SKILLS, DRILLS AND PRACTICES: BOWLING

Whether you are working with seam bowlers or spinners, bowlers have two main roles: to take wickets and to restrict runs. But while their objective is the same, even among similar bowlers – for example, right-arm medium pacers – no two bowlers are exactly alike, and this individuality should be encouraged when coaching bowling. Some of the best bowlers in world cricket have unique actions that you won't find in any coaching manual but which have proved to be devastatingly effective.

When observing your bowlers, the most important things to consider – as in all your coaching – are simply, is it safe? – that is, unlikely to cause injury – and is it effective? – meaning, is the outcome what we are looking for? If the answer to these two questions is 'yes', then don't worry if the action you are observing isn't a textbook version of a bowling action. However, just as with batting, there are many traits that bowlers share. From a smooth, rhythmical run-up, to staying balanced and keeping their energy going towards the target, these basics are key in helping youngsters learn the art of bowling.

There are three main action types: side-on, front-on and mid-way. These refer to the alignment of the hips and shoulders to the target at the point of back-foot contact. When teaching beginners how to bowl for the first time you should encourage them to use the side-on action. This is because it puts the least stress on a growing body, and

is easier for children to master. However, if you have a player in your squad who naturally bowls front-on or mid-way they should be encouraged to keep bowling this way.

The Bowling Process

It can be useful to break down the bowling process into six main areas: run-up, take-off, back foot contact, front foot contact and point of release, and follow-through.

Run-up
Whatever type of bowler you are coaching, all will need a smooth, rhythmical run-up. Typically, a spin bowler's run-up will be shorter and slower than a seamer's. But while the length, speed and angle of the run-up may differ, the key points are largely the same whether you are working with a fast bowler or a spinner. The bowler's approach should be the same length and speed each time – even the foot they start on should be the same. Their run-up should go in a straight line towards the target, and should ensure they reach the crease in a balanced, upright position.

Young seam bowlers will often try and run in too fast, which causes them to lose rhythm. The ideal running style should look more like a 400m runner than a 100m sprinter, and bowlers should accelerate slightly as they get closer to take-off.

Take-off

The take-off is the transition between the run-up and the bowling action. For right-arm bowlers it involves jumping from your left foot. For left-handers it involves taking off on your right foot.

Just like the other phases of bowling, it is important that the player remains balanced, with their head still and eyes level. As the bowler takes off they should continue moving towards their target and start bringing their arms into position to bowl. It is important that their arms remain close to their body to avoid losing momentum. Side-on bowlers will need to rotate their body while they are in the air to ensure they are in the right position on back foot contact.

Back foot contact

Back foot contact is the point when the bowler lands following their take-off. Right-handed bowlers should land on their right foot, while left-armers should land on their left. Side-on bowlers should land with their foot parallel to the crease, front-on bowlers with their toes pointing down the pitch, and mid-way bowlers half way between the two. Their hips and shoulders should be aligned as described in the action types text box. For both off-spin and leg-spin bowlers, the side-on action is the most effective action type.

While bowlers will bend their back leg slightly on landing, they should try to stay as tall as possible. Their front arm should come up so that their elbow is at least level with their shoulder. They should be in a balanced position, with their eyes level, looking over their left shoulder at the target (side-on) or inside it (front-on).

Front foot contact and point of release

The front foot should land with the toes pointing down the wicket at the target. The front arm should pull down past the front hip as the bowling arm comes up to release the ball. Keeping their arm straight, bowlers should release the ball from the equivalent of an eleven o'clock position on a clock face, although this can vary slightly. Seam bowlers should have their wrist behind the ball, while for spinners this is the point where spin is imparted on to the ball (see next section 'Grips'). The front leg should be straight with the knee braced. The bowler should remain balanced with their eyes level, looking towards their target.

Follow-through

The follow-through refers to the phase of the bowling action after the bowler has released the ball. This differs for seamers and spinners.

For seamers

After releasing the ball, both arms should swing through powerfully past the front hip. At the same the back leg should drive towards the target. The momentum generated from the bowling action should push the bowler down the wicket towards the target. They should keep going until they stop naturally, rather than 'pulling up'. They should stay balanced throughout.

For spinners

Instead of travelling down the wicket towards the target, spinners should pivot on their front foot through 180 degrees after releasing the ball. This means that right-armers will finish with their right side nearest the batsman, and vice versa for left-handers. They should remain tall and balanced throughout.

Grips

Seam

The basic grip for seam bowlers is to hold the ball with their index and middle fingers running along the seam, which should be vertical. The side of the thumb should be in contact with the underside of the seam. For in-swing and away-swing grips, see the section on swing later in this chapter.

Off spin

* An off spinner will turn the ball from off to leg – or in to a right-handed batsman.

Off spinners hold the ball with a horizontal seam and grip it between their first two fingers. Their third and fourth fingers should be pointing down, and their thumb should not be in contact with the ball. Young players may have their third finger touching the ball for control, but this should be avoided if possible as it will reduce the amount of spin they can produce. Spin is imparted by the action of the first finger and through turning your wrist

An off spin bowler in action. 1. Take off. 2. In mid air. 3. Back foot contact.

An off spin bowler in action. 4. Point of release. 5 & 6. Follow through.

clockwise like opening a door. Off spin is also referred to as finger spin because it is the use of the fingers that creates the revolutions on the ball. This grip and action on the ball is the same for left-arm spinners.

Leg spin

- A leg spinner will turn the ball from leg to off – or away from a right-handed batsman.

Leg spinners hold the ball with the seam in a horizontal position and the top joints of their first two fingers across it. The third finger is in a bent position and their thumb should be off the ball. Spin is imparted by the third finger and a flick of the wrist. The wrist should turn anti-clockwise so the ball comes out of the back of the hand. The grip and action on the ball is the same for left-arm leg spinners.

Leg spin bowler in action. 1 & 2. Take off. 3. Front foot contact. 4. Just after point of release.

Leg spin bowler in action (continued). 5. Follow through

Bowling Practices

Target Bowling

Aim: To develop accuracy using the basic bowling action.

Equipment: One set of stumps, one ball and five cones per group.

Number of players: Three to six.

Explanation: Mark out a pitch (full length if using a hard ball, around 10m if using a tennis ball) with a set of stumps at one end and a cone at the other. Place a wicketkeeper behind the stumps and the bowlers behind the cone.

Mark out a target area about 1m wide and 2m long, about 1.5m in front of the stumps.

Bowlers take it in turns to bowl, aiming for the target. After bowling their ball they replace the wicketkeeper. The wicketkeeper collects the ball and brings it back to the next bowler before joining the back of the queue. This is then repeated for each player.

Bowlers get one point for landing the ball in the target zone, and another for hitting the stumps. These points can count towards a team or individual competition.

Make it harder: *Make the target area smaller. *Increase the distance from the target (if not already using a full pitch). *Remove one or more stumps.

Make it easier: *Increase the size of the target area. *Bowl from the base (standing) position. *Add another set of stumps.

INTRODUCING SPIN

Coaches are often a little reticent to coach spin as it is seen as a very specialist skill or almost as some kind of 'dark art' among those who don't bowl it themselves. However, I believe it is something that you should encourage all your bowlers to try.

When coaching spin the main emphasis should be on getting players to spin the ball as much as possible – we can teach control later!

A good way to introduce spin is to get players to use the grips described above, but to practise spinning the ball underarm in pairs. If you have a line on a sports hall floor or a line of cones you can encourage your players to practise spinning the ball from one side of the line to the other. Once they have mastered the skill underarm you can move on to throwing from the elbow, throwing with a full action, and eventually bowling from the base (standing) position.

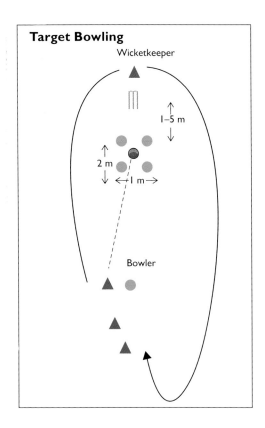

Target Bowling

Wicketkeeper

1–5 m

2 m

←1 m→

Bowler

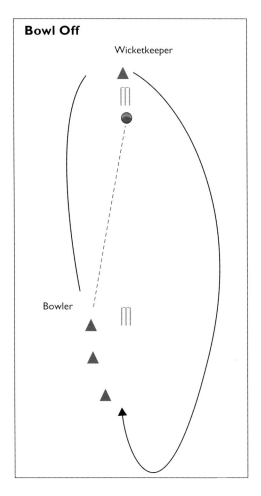

Bowl Off

Wicketkeeper

Bowler

Top tip: Encourage players to keep their heads up and eyes level by placing a batting tee on top of the off stump. They should keep their eye on this throughout the bowling action.

Bowl Off

Aim: To develop accuracy under pressure using the basic bowling action.

Equipment: One set of stumps, one ball and one cone.

Number of players: Three to six.

Explanation: Set up the practice as for target bowling but without the scoring zone. This time the aim is simply to hit the stumps.

Every time a bowler hits the wickets they remove a stump until there are none left to hit.

This works best as a competition with other teams, but it can also be done against the clock.

Make it harder: *Increase the distance from the target (if not already using a full pitch). *Players have to hit the stumps in order – for example off stump, then middle, then leg. *Decrease the time they are allowed to hit the stumps in.

Make it easier: *Add a second set of stumps next to the first so the target is bigger. *Bowl from the base (standing) position. *Make the pitch shorter.

Top tip: Encourage players to follow through in a straight line towards the target. This can be a channel marked with cones or lines on a sports-hall floor.

Take-off and Landing

Aim: To develop the take-off and landing phase of the bowling action (also known as 'the bound').

Equipment: One stump and two bases or a small hurdle, one ball and two cones per group.

Number of players: Two to six.

Explanation: Set up the practice with a wicketkeeper behind a cone at one end, and the bowlers just over a pitch length away behind a second cone. Just before the point where the players bowl from, place the hurdle. If you don't have a hurdle, a plastic

Take-off and Landing

Wicketkeeper

Hurdle

Bowler

stump suspended between two bases is just as good.

Taking it in turns, the bowlers must step over the hurdle using the bound before bowling the ball to the wicketkeeper. To develop this phase of the action, players need to place their *non*-bowling foot (left for right armers and right for left armers) just in front of the hurdle. The bowling foot then steps over the cones and lands parallel to the bowling crease, and the player then completes the bowling action and bowls. Thus the sequence of feet for a *right*-arm bowler is: take off on the *left* foot, land on the *right* foot, bowl from the *left* foot.

Make it harder: *Balance the stump between the bases so the player has to avoid knocking it off. *Incorporate target-bowling or bowl-off practices. *Include a full run-up.

Make it easier: *Do the practice without a ball until players have grasped the basic technique. *Players may walk through the bound before trying to jump. *Instead of a hurdle use a line of small cones.

Top tip: Tell the players to say which foot they are landing on as they do the practice – thus for a right arm bowler 'Left, right, left,' as they go through the sequence. If they are struggling to distinguish left and right, tell them to roll up one trouser leg above the knee to help them.

Bowling Corridor

Aim: To develop the run-up and transfer of energy towards the target.

Equipment: One ball, eight cones (minimum), one set of stumps per group.

Number of players: Two to six.

Bowling Corridor

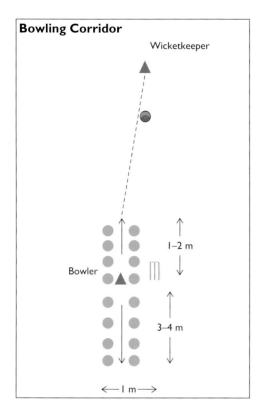

Explanation: Set up the practice as for target bowling, but with the stumps at the bowler's end, and without a scoring zone. Instead place a 1m-wide 'corridor' of cones alongside the bowler's end stumps. The channel should start 3–4m back from the wickets and finish 2–3m past the bowling crease to cover their approach to the wicket, the point of release, and the start of the follow-through. Each bowler takes it in turns to run through the channel and bowl the ball to the wicket-keeper. They should look to keep their whole body in the corridor throughout their action.

Make it harder: *Replace the cones with stumps, intervention poles, or bamboo canes (depending on what you have available) so that the corridor comes above waist height.

*Incorporate target-bowling or bowl-off practices. *Make the corridor narrower.

Make it easier: *Make the corridor wider. *Use the cones for the approach only, and not for the follow-through. *Start by walking through the corridor rather than running.

Top tip: Encourage players to use an athletic running style, with their head upright and arms moving in an efficient way, staying close the body.

Hit the Cones

Aim: To develop accuracy and control while bowling.

Equipment: One ball and thirteen cones per group (stumps optional).

Number of players: Three to six.

Hit the Cones

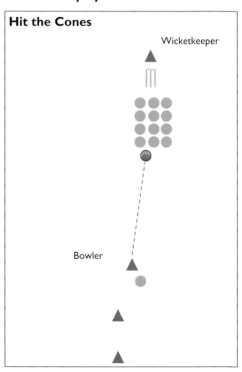

Explanation: Set up the practice as for target bowling, but instead of a scoring zone place the twelve cones on different lines and lengths. You may decide that they should all be in one place – for example, on or just outside off stump on a good length – or they can be placed at random.

The aim is to hit the cones. Each time a bowler does this a cone is taken away. You can continue the practice until all the cones have been hit, or run it against the clock.

Make it harder: *Nominate which cone a player should aim for prior to bowling. *Spread the cones out, or use fewer. *Give the players a specific game scenario and tell them to place the cones where they would bowl in this situation.

Make it easier: *Use larger cones, or use more. *Bowl from the base (standing) position. *Make the pitch shorter.

Top tip: Discuss with players how to adjust their aim. For example, if a bowler normally looks at the base of off stump, they may need to look at the top to bowl fuller. If they want to bowl shorter they may need to choose a spot on the pitch to look at.

Bowling at the Death
Aim: To develop the yorker, a skill that is particularly useful at the end of an innings.

Equipment: One ball, a cone and three plastic stump bases per group.

Number of players: Three to six.

Explanation: Set up the practice as for the bowl-off practice but instead of a set of stumps, place the three plastic bases on top of each other. The wicketkeeper will need

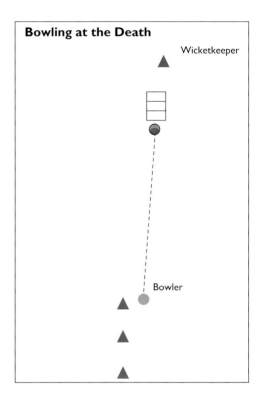

Bowling at the Death

Wicketkeeper

Bowler

to be slightly further back than for the other practices.

Taking it in turns, the bowlers aim to try and hit the bases, getting the ball to bounce just in front of them. Each time they do this they are awarded ten points.

As with the other drills, this can be run as a head-to-head competition between teams, or individuals.

Make it harder: *Use fewer bases. *Turn the bases so that the narrower end is facing the bowler, making a smaller target. *Take away points if the ball hits the bases without bouncing.

Make it easier: *Use more bases. *Place a small target zone in front of the bases and award five points if the ball lands in it. *Make the pitch shorter.

Top tip: Encourage players to look beyond their target and imagine transferring extra energy to the ball at the point of release.

Off Spin

Aim: To develop accuracy and generate spin using the off-spin action.

Equipment: One ball, a cone, a full set of stumps, one base with off stump in only, and another with leg-stump only.

Number of players: Three to six.

Explanation: Set up the practice as for the bowl-off practice with a wicketkeeper behind the stumps and a group of bowlers behind a cone one pitch length away (or about 10m if using a tennis ball).

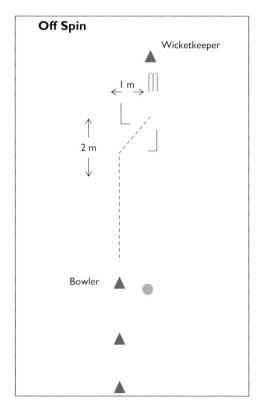

Place the base with the off stump in line with the batting crease and about 1m outside off stump. Place the base with the other single stump so that the leg stump is in line with the middle of the full set of stumps, about 2m from the batting crease.

The players should bowl the ball, and using off spin, attempt to spin it between the two single stumps. They get ten points every time they are successful.

Make it harder: *Make the gap between the single stumps narrower. *Only award points if the ball also hits the stumps. *Make the distance between the single stumps shorter.

Make it easier: *Make the distance between the two single stumps longer in length. *Bowl underarm or from the base position. *Award five points for any ball that spins even if it doesn't go through the 'goal' made by the single stumps.

Top tip: It is important for spinners to make sure they are aligned to the target when they bowl. For off spinners this means having their hips and shoulders in line with the off stump. A great way to practise this is to tie a piece of string from the off stump at the batsman's end to the place the bowler releases the ball from – for example half way between the stumps and the return crease. Bowling from the base position, bowlers should try to start and finish their action on the string to ensure they stay aligned to the target.

Leg Spin

Aim: To develop accuracy and generate spin using the leg-spin action.

Equipment: One ball, a cone, a full set of stumps, one base with off stump in only and another with leg stump only.

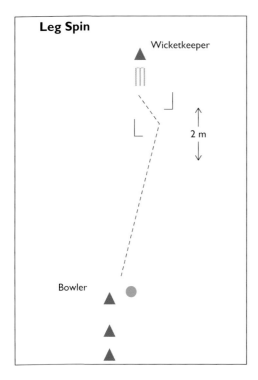

Number of players: Three to six.

Explanation: Set up the practice as for the off-spin practice but with the 'goal' set up to encourage leg spin.

Place the base with the leg stump in line with the batting crease and about one wicket's width outside leg stump. Place the base with the off stump so it lines up with the off stump of the full set of stumps, about 2m from the batting crease.

The players should bowl the ball, and using leg spin, attempt to spin it between the two single stumps. They get ten points every time they are successful.

Make it harder: *Make the gap between the single stumps narrower. *Only award points if the ball also hits the stumps. *Make the distance between the single stumps shorter.

Make it easier: *Make the distance between the two single stumps longer. *Bowl underarm or from the base position. *Award five points for any ball that spins even if it doesn't go through the 'goal' made by the single stumps.

Top tip: Repeat the alignent practice as for off spin, but tie the string from middle stump/ middle and leg on the stumps at the batsman's end.

Spin Flight Practice
Aim: To help spin bowlers develop the art of flight.

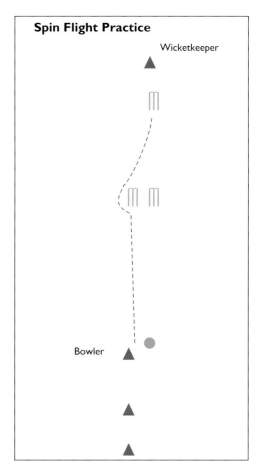

Equipment: One ball, a cone, three full sets of stumps.

Number of players: Three to six.

Explanation: Set up the practice as for the bowl off, but place two sets of stumps side by side halfway down the pitch.

Bowling either leg spin or off spin, players should bowl the ball over the double set of stumps and try to get it to bounce before reaching the wicket. They get ten points every time they are successful.

Make it harder: *Make the gap between the double stumps and the stumps at the batsman's end smaller. *Add a target box outside off stump for off spinners, and covering the area between middle stump and just outside leg stump for leg spinners. *Deduct points if players hit the double set of stumps.

Make it easier: *Make the distance between the double stumps and the stumps at the batsman's end bigger. *Bowl from the base position. *Use a shorter obstacle in place of the double stumps.

Top tip: Place a visual target, such as a ball on top of a batting tee, on top of the batsman's stumps for the spinners to look at when bowling. This will stop them becoming too distracted by the double stumps, and will help them find a good length.

Traffic Lights

Aim: To help bowlers – both seamers and spinners – develop control and decision making.

Equipment: One ball, a set of stumps and twelve cones – four red, four yellow and four green.

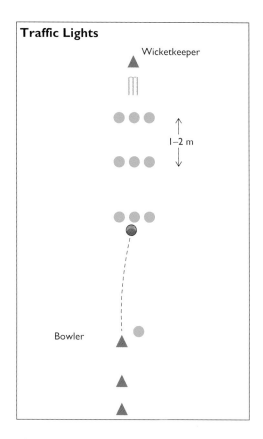

Traffic Lights

Wicketkeeper

1–2 m

Bowler

Number of players: Three to six.

Explanation: Set up the practice as for the bowl off, but place three green cones just in front of the batting crease, three yellow cones 1–2m further back towards the bowler's end and three red cones another 1–2m further back. One player stands behind the cone at the bowler's end holding the other three cones.

As the bowler runs in, the player at the bowler's end holds out one of the cones. The bowler needs to try to hit the cones that match the one held out. If no cone is held out they must aim for the stumps. They get ten points every time they hit their intended target.

Each bowler should have three goes in a row before swapping.

Make it harder: *Use one or two cones only for each target. *Delay holding out the cones until just before the bowler takes off. *Mix up the colours – for example, the bowler has to hit the yellow cones when the green cone is held out.

Make it easier: *Make the targets bigger. *Give the bowler more time to see the cone held out. *Let the bowler choose which cones they will hit before bowling.

Top tip: The position of the cones should relate to a yorker length, a good length and a short length. Make sure you discuss with your bowlers when and why they may look to bowl different lengths at different points during a game.

Swing

Swing is the term given to the lateral movement of the ball through the air after release. The ball can swing from the leg side towards the off side – away swing – or from off to leg – in swing.

Swing is caused by the way the bowler grips the ball and the position of their wrist at the point of release, but it can be affected by a wide range of different factors: the seam position, the state of the ball, the weather conditions and the tide. Some people say even the number of trees at a ground can have an impact on how much the ball swings. Clearly some of these factors are impossible to control so you should advise your bowlers to focus on the ones they can influence, namely the state of the ball and the position of the seam.

The Ball
To maximize the amount of swing they can produce players should work on the ball to make sure one side is shiny and the other is allowed to scuff up naturally – this is why you see bowlers constantly polishing the ball on their trousers. The best way to shine a ball is to rub saliva into the ball and rub it hard on your clothing. To get a ball really shiny, the side you polish should be almost warm to the touch after shining it. If the ball remains damp to the touch it is unlikely to swing.

Grip
Most swing bowlers will have subtle differences in the way they hold the ball, based on everything from hand size to what feels comfortable for them. While you should encourage your players to find a grip that works for them, there are a few basics that will help them on their way.

Away swing: For the ball to swing away from a right-handed batsman the bowler needs to hold the ball with the basic grip, but should angle the seam slightly towards the off side. The bowler should also make sure the scuffed side is on the off side, and the ball is held in the ends of the fingers. The side of the thumb should remain in contact with the seam underneath.

In swing: To make the ball swing in, replicate the grip above but angle the seam towards the leg side and make sure the scuffed side is also on the leg side. In-swing bowlers normally have the flat of their thumb on the underside of the seam.

Swing can also be influenced by action types: thus side-on bowlers tend to find it easier to swing the ball away from right-handers, while front-on bowlers more naturally swing the ball in. However, the very best bowlers are able to swing the ball both ways from the same action by adjusting the grip as above.

Practise swinging the ball

A great way for young bowlers to practise swinging the ball is to take a tennis ball and cover one side with masking tape. This will act as the shiny side and help get bowlers used to producing and controlling swing.

SEAM MOVEMENT

Being able to get the ball to swing or move off the seam are vital weapons in a seam bowler's armoury. While 'seam bowlers' is a collective term used to describe all bowlers who aren't spinners, 'seam' is also a type of lateral movement that can be a key weapon in getting batsmen out.

The main difference between seam and swing is that seam movement happens off the pitch rather than through the air. It is caused by the seam of the ball hitting the pitch at an angle, which can make it move into a batsman or away from them. Skilful bowlers can exaggerate this movement by running their fingers across the seam at the point of release. This is known as bowling 'cutters'.

For young bowlers, however, I wouldn't worry about this skill too much. Instead, get them to run in with the away-swing and in-swing grips described above. If the ball doesn't swing through the air there is still a good chance it will move off the pitch if the seam is in the right position.

As well as being influenced by grip, seam movement can be affected by how much grass is on the pitch, and also by the state of the ball – for instance a new ball will move more than an old one, as the seam will be harder and more pronounced.

A seam bowler in action. 1. Take off. 2. Front foot contact. 3. Just before point of release. 4. Follow through.

CHAPTER 8

SKILLS, DRILLS AND PRACTICES: FIELDING AND WICKETKEEPING

In modern times fielding has become an increasingly valued and vital part of the game. Good fielding can put the batting team under pressure by reducing scoring, and can help take wickets through catches and run-outs. Most players will spend more time fielding in a game than anything else. Therefore it is important that we, as coaches, prioritize fielding practice, make sure our players enjoy it, and help them develop a wide range of skills so they become a real asset to the team.

Many coaches are slightly fearful of coaching wicketkeeping as it is a specialist position. But it is important that we offer all our young players the chance to try their hand at it, because not only will this help you find out who your best keepers are, but many of the skills are transferable to other parts of cricket.

Fielding Positions

Although there are a large number of fielding positions, they can be categorized into three main areas: close catchers, ring fielders and boundary fielders.

Close catchers
Close catchers include slip and gully fielders, and players in catching positions in front of the wicket, such as short leg. The main purpose of these fielders is to take catches that come their way. Typically the ball will come hard and low, which means that players in these positions need quick reactions and excellent close-catching skills. They will also need to concentrate for long periods as they do not tend to field the ball that often, but when they do it is often crucial – for example, an outside edge that carries to first slip.

Key skills: Close catch.

Ring fielders
'Ring fielders' is the general term given to players who field in positions such as cover, point, square leg, midwicket, mid-on and mid-off. During a game they may have to perform a wide range of different roles, including cutting off quick singles, stopping balls that have been hit hard towards the boundary, and taking catches. They will also need to back up other fielders and chase any balls hit past them, and they may be called upon to attempt a run-out.

Key skills: One-hand and two-hand pick-ups, overarm and underarm throw, skim catch, high catch, turn and throw.

Boundary fielders
The main job of a boundary fielder is to protect the boundary, as the name suggests. It includes positions such as fine leg, third man, deep cover, deep backward square leg, long-on and long-off. Boundary fielders may be called upon to stop powerfully struck shots going for four, to run in to stop batsmen running a two, or to take high catches.

Key skills: Overarm throw, two-handed pick-up, crow hop, skim catch, high catch.

Close Catch

Description: Close catchers (see above) must catch the ball safely when it reaches them at around waist height or below.

Coaching points:
- Players should stand in a balanced position with their legs about shoulder-width apart, their knees bent and their weight on the balls of their feet.
- They should be leaning forwards with their head over their feet, eyes level.

Close catch. Fielders should be in a balanced position and catch the ball with their fingers pointing down.

- They should catch the ball with their little fingers together, finger tips pointing down.
- They should 'give' with their hands as they receive the ball to stop the ball bouncing out of their hands.

Top tip: When coaching young players, tell them to think of how a football goalkeeper stands for a penalty: their starting position is very similar to the stance for the close catch.

Practice drill for the close catch
Aim: To catch the ball safely using the close catch technique.

Equipment: One ball per pair, with cones to mark the space.

Number of players: Two to thirty.

Explanation: Divide players into twos, with one ball per pair. Players should stand about 4m away from each other and throw the ball underarm, aiming to get it at waist height or lower.

When players can do this successfully, time them to see how many catches they can take as a pair in one minute.

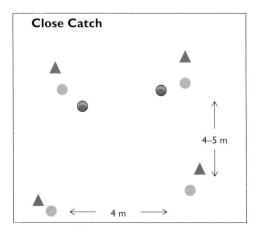

Close Catch

4–5 m

4 m

Finally, bring two pairs together and position players so they face their partner diagonally across a 4m-4m square marked out with cones.

Repeat the practice above, but this time players have the additional distraction of another ball in their eyeline.

Make it harder: *Make players go back to 0 if they drop the ball. *Give each player a ball each (two per pair), and get them throwing simultaneously. *Add more pairs at the end so there are more balls in the catcher's eyeline.

Make it easier: *Make the distance between players smaller. *Use a bigger ball. *Allow players to catch the ball after it has bounced.

High catch
Description: This skill is a method of catching the ball safely when it has been hit high in the air and reaches the player above waist height.

Coaching points:
- Players should move underneath the ball and get themselves in a balanced position with their legs about shoulder-width apart, knees slightly bent and head steady.
- They should bring their hands together at eye level, and catch with their little fingers together and hands parallel to the ground.
- They should take the catch at eye level and 'give' with their hands by bringing the ball into the chest.

Top tip: Where possible, encourage your players to get under the ball as quickly as possible so they can make sure they are in a stable, balanced position when they catch.

Taking a high catch.

Practice drill for high catching

Aim: To develop the high catch technique using a series of fun challenges.

Equipment: One ball per player

Number of players: As many as you have space and balls for.

Explanation: Each player is given one ball and asked to find a space. By throwing the ball above their head and using the high catch technique, players are given the following challenges one at a time:

- See how high they can throw the ball and still catch it
- See how many claps they can make before catching the ball: start with one clap and increase by one each time they catch the ball
- Throw the ball up and touch their nose before catching. If this is achieved, repeat but touch nose and ears. Repeat as above for nose, ears, belly, knees and finally feet. Players still need to touch each body part each time

Make it harder/easier: The beauty of these challenges is that players will naturally find their own level, and therefore you shouldn't need to add progressions or simplify the drill.

Skim Catch/Reverse Hands High Catch

Description: The skim catch or reverse hands is the technique commonly used by fielders in all positions when the ball is travelling towards them at chest height or above. It can be used for a ball travelling at a flat trajectory, or to take a high catch where the ball is moving towards them.

Coaching points:

- Players should stand with their feet about shoulder-width apart, with the knees slightly bent
- They should catch the ball using reversed hands (see pic on next page), so the palms face the ball, with the fingers pointing up and the thumbs crossed or together
- Players should aim to take the catch at about eye level where possible, and should give with their hands to bring the ball in towards their shoulder

Top tip: Try to encourage fielders to take the ball slightly in front of them so they can take the impact of the ball. Remember, when this technique is used the ball is travelling towards the player, often at speed.

Practice drill for taking a skim catch

Equipment: One tennis ball, one tennis racquet, and three cones per group. (If using a hard ball, you will need to hit with a cricket bat.)

Number of players: Groups of two to three.

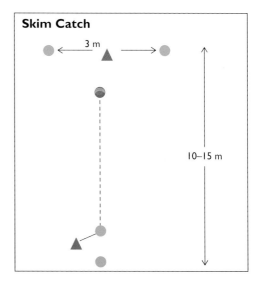

Skim Catch

3 m

10–15 m

Taking a skim catch.

Explanation: Using two cones, create a 'goal' about 3m wide. Place the other cone about 10–15m away in a straight line.

One player stands in the goal, the other stands by the other cone and uses the tennis racquet to hit balls to them at about shoulder height with a flat trajectory.

If the fielder catches the ball they score a point. If the player drops it, or it goes into the goal, then the hitter scores a point. Each player has six goes before swapping.

For this to work you will have to ensure your players have the control to hit the ball where you want it. You will also need to make sure they only score points if the balls they hit are between waist and head height.

To practise the reverse hands high catch, repeat the practice but make the goals wider, move them further back, and change the feed so that it goes higher and drops as it reaches the fielder.

Make it harder: *Make the goal wider. *Increase the power of the feed. *Alternate the trajectory of the feed to practise the skim catch and reverse hands high catch.

Make it easier: *Tell the feeder to throw the ball rather than hit it. *Make the goal smaller. *Remove the scoring.

Overarm Throw

Description: The overarm throw is used by fielders in the ring and on the boundary. It can be used to limit the number of runs a batsman can score, or to attempt a run-out.

Coaching points:

- Players should turn side on to the target (left side nearest the target for right handers and vice versa for left handers), and take a long stride towards it with the back foot at 90 degrees.
- They should point their front arm at the

target and pull back their throwing arm to make an L shape so that the elbow is level or above the shoulder.

- Keeping their head still and eyes level, they should throw the ball powerfully, finishing chest on to the target.
- As they throw, the non-throwing arm should drive past the front hip.
- After release, the throwing arm should follow through across the chest and the back foot should be dragged forwards to finish level with the front one.

Top tip: Encourage players to throw from a wide base with their feet as far apart as is comfortable. This will ensure they are using their leg muscles to help throw, which will increase power.

Practice drill for the overarm throw

Aim: To develop a powerful, accurate throw in a fun team practice.

Equipment: At least one ball per two players. At least one set of stumps per six players. Four to twenty cones depending on numbers.

Number of players: Two to thirty, depending on space and equipment.

Explanation: This game can be played in pairs or small groups, but works best as a team game with between twelve and thirty players.

Take as many sets of stumps as you have, and place them between the two teams, about 10m from each group. The sets should be equally spaced apart. The players stand behind a line of cones and have a ball each, or one between two.

When the coach shouts 'go' the players throw overarm at the stumps – remaining behind the cones at all times. If they knock the stumps over it is a point to their team.

Overarm throw.

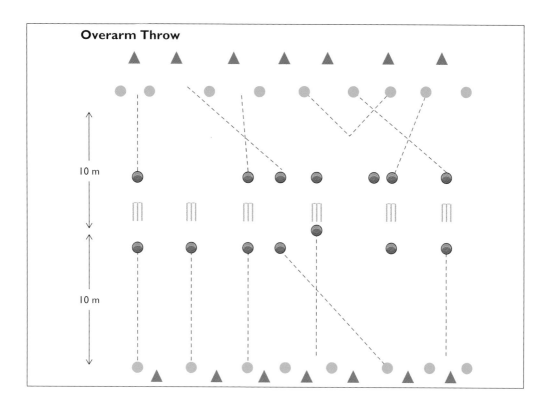

The game continues until all the stumps have been knocked over.

If doing this as a small group game with a single set of stumps, you can pick the stumps back up after each hit and play over a certain time period.

Make it harder: *Take out one or two stumps from each set to decrease the size of the target. *Make the throwers stand further away. *Deduct points if fielders misfield the balls thrown by the other team.

Make it easier: *Place the stumps next to each other without any gaps to create a bigger target. *Decrease the distance players throw from. *Players don't have to knock stumps over, simply hitting them is enough to score a point.

One-hand Intercept and Underarm Throw

Description: The one-hand intercept and underarm throw is a fast, dynamic skill used by fielders in the ring to cut off quick singles and/or attempt a run-out. It is used when the ball is within about 10m from the stumps and rolling along the ground.

Coaching points:
- Players should attack the ball at speed in a balanced position, low to the ground.
- They should pick up the ball outside their throwing foot, with fingers pointing down and palm facing the ball.
- When throwing they should point their non-throwing arm at the target and keep their head still, looking at where they are throwing.

READY POSITION AND 'WALKING IN'

Just like the stance in batting, fielders also need to make sure they are in a prime position to react to the ball. The ready position allows players to get into a balanced, athletic position from which they can move in any direction: it is similar to a football goalkeeper or a tennis player at the net, and is particularly important for players fielding in the ring.

Coaching points:
- Players should begin by 'walking in' towards the striker's end as the bowler runs in.
- Fielders should be light on their feet and in a slightly crouched, balanced position.
- Just before the ball is bowled the fielder should make a small jump and 'split-step' movement: this puts them in an athletic position with legs apart and their weight on the balls of their feet.

Top tip: Encourage players to follow through (keep running) towards the target after they have thrown, to help the ball go straight.

Practice Drill for One-hand Intercept and Underarm Throw

One-hand Intercept and Underarm Throw

Aim: To develop the one-hand intercept and underarm throw in a competitive 'run-out' race versus batters.

Equipment: One ball, one bat, one set of stumps and five cones.

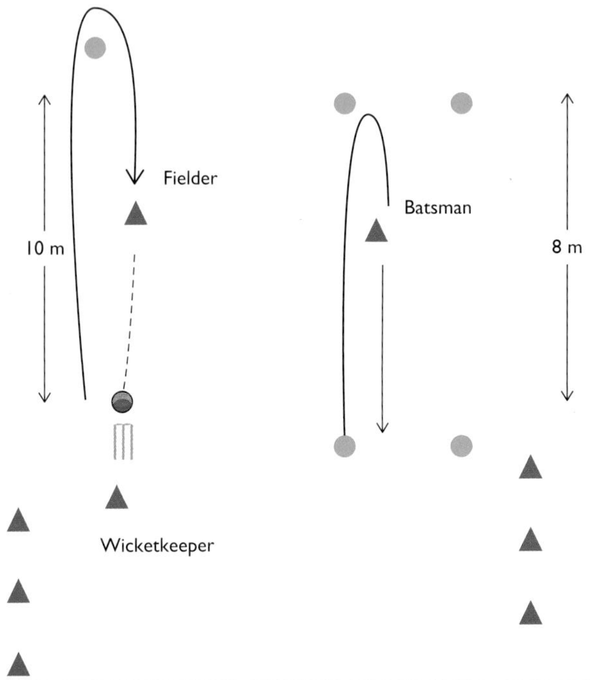

Number of players: Up to twelve.

Explanation: Divide the players into two equal groups: one will begin as batters, the other as fielders. The batters line up behind a cone facing a 'goal' of two cones 8m away; the fielders line up next to a set of stumps alongside the batters. A wicketkeeper stands behind the stumps with a ball. Opposite the stumps, about 2m further away than the batters 'goal', is a single cone.

When the coach shouts 'go', the first batter and fielder sprint out. The batter runs their bat between the two cones of the 'goal' and sprints back. The fielder runs around their cone, and on the way back fields a ball that has been rolled out by the wicketkeeper

One-hand intercept and underarm throw.

using the one-hand pick-up and underarm throw.

If the batter gets back before the ball, it's a point to their team. If the ball goes to the wicketkeeper and they knock the bails off before the batter returns, it's a point to the fielders. Direct hits do not count. Players swap groups after having two goes each.

Make it harder: *Make the distance further for the fielders. *Make players use their weaker hand. *Use a reaction ball.

Make it easier: *Use a stationary ball. *The throw just has to go into the wicketkeeper's hands, rather than taking off the bails. *Make the distances shorter.

Turn and Throw

Description: The turn and throw is used by fielders in the ring when the ball has been hit past them and they need to cut it off and return it to the wicketkeeper or bowler.

Coaching points:
* The fielder should chase the ball on a line slightly to the non-throwing side of the ball.
* As they near the ball they get low to the ground.
* The fielder should slightly overrun the ball and pick up in their throwing hand, just outside their throwing foot.
* Taking the weight on their throwing leg, they should push back towards the target and establish a firm base by stepping towards the target. They then return the ball to the wicket-keeper using the over-arm throw.

Top tip: Make sure players take a big stride back towards the target after picking up the ball; this will create a stable, balanced base and improve accuracy.

Practice drill for turn and throw
Aim: To develop the turn and throw under the pressure of a competitive practice.

Equipment: One ball, two cones, and a set of stumps per team.

Description: Divide the group into equal teams, with a wicketkeeper behind each set of stumps. Place one cone about 15m from the wicketkeeper and the other 5m further on.

When the coach shouts 'go', the wicketkeepers roll the ball between the two cones and the fielders sprint out and perform the turn and throw, returning the ball to the wicketkeeper. As soon as the wicketkeeper receives the ball they roll it out for the next player, who repeats the drill. The first team to have been through twice each is the winner.

Make it harder: *Increase the distance. *Throw the balls out on an angle. *Use a reaction ball.

Make it easier: *Use stationary balls. *Decrease the distance. *Remove the competitive element.

Two-handed Pick-up and Crow-hop

Description: The two-handed pick-up and crow-hop is an attacking skill used by fielders on the edge of the ring or out in the deep. The skill allows them to pick up the ball at speed, and to create a stable base to throw from without losing any momentum.

Coaching points:
* Players should attack the ball at speed in a balanced position, low to the ground.
* As they approach the ball they should start to turn their body side on so they

Practising the turn and throw.

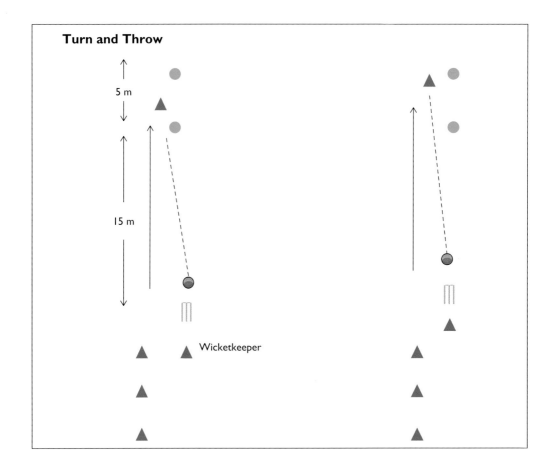

Turn and Throw

5 m

15 m

Wicketkeeper

can pick it up in front of the instep of their throwing foot.

- As the player stands up they should bring their throwing foot behind their non-throwing foot (or in front, if this is more comfortable) before taking a stride towards the target.
- They complete the skill by performing the overarm throw.

Top tip: Start by using a stationary ball and walking through the movement. You can also place flat markers on the ground to show where each step should take place.

Practice drill for two-handed pick-up and crow-hop

Aim: To develop the two-handed pick-up and crow-hop in a competitive practice.

Equipment: One ball, one set of stumps, and one cone per group.

Number of players: Up to six per group.

Explanation: Divide the group into equal teams. Each team should have a wicketkeeper behind a set of stumps. The rest of the team should be lined up behind a cone about 20m from the wicket-keeper.

Two-handed pick-up and crow-hop.

Two-handed pick-up and crow-hop (continued).

The wicketkeeper rolls the ball out, and the fielders take it in turns to field the ball using the two-handed pick-up, crow-hop and over-arm throw. After throwing they join the back of the queue.

Each player goes twice, and the team that finishes first is the winner.

Make it harder: *Make the distance longer. *Roll out the ball on different angles. *Use a reaction ball.

Make it easier: *Use a stationary ball. *Make the distance shorter. *Let the players walk through the movement.

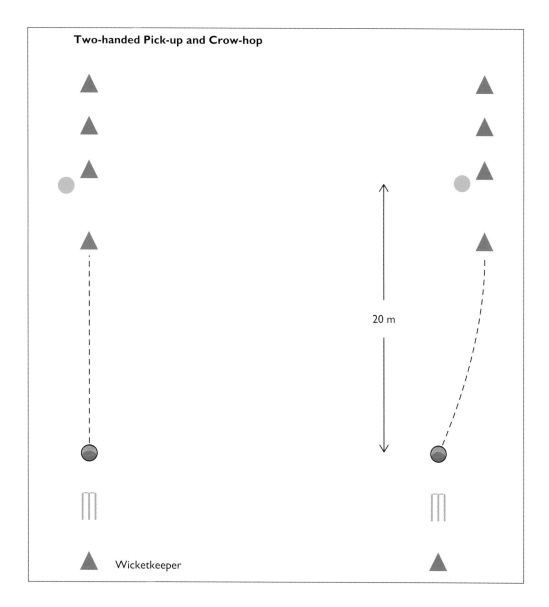

Two-handed Pick-up and Crow-hop

20 m

Wicketkeeper

Wicketkeeper's stance: front view.

Wicketkeeper's stance: side view.

Wicketkeeping

The wicketkeeper is one of the most important members of any team, but because it is a specialist position many coaches often neglect them in their practices. More often than not the wicketkeeper is used to help coaches run fielding drills for their team-mates, rather than having the opportunity to focus specifically on their own skills.

As players get older they will begin to specialize their skills, but it is important that we don't put our players into boxes too soon. I believe all players should be given the opportunity to take part in wicketkeeping practices at a young age. Children tend to really enjoy these 'keeping drills, and it can also compliment their catching and coordination skills.

When coaching 'keeping we should remember that we are looking for an agile player who is light on their feet, has good hands, and is equally comfortable standing up to the stumps or standing back.

For both standing up and standing back the initial stance is very similar, but wicketkeepers may be slightly lower to the ground when standing up.

Coaching points:
- Players should squat with their feet about shoulder-width apart, and their weight on the balls of their feet.
- Their hands should be together and slightly in front of the body, with the fingers pointing down.
- The head should be still, the eyes level.

Below are a few simple drills to get your players started, and there are any number of ways you can adapt these simple practices

Wicketkeeper's stance: side view.

- The player's body should 'come up' as they take the ball, and they should 'give' with their hands.

If the ball is on the off side or leg side the player should repeat as above, but will first need to move in line with the ball using small side steps, remaining balanced at all times.

Top tip: Tell players to practise their footwork by setting up a 'goal' made of two cones about 4m apart with the 'keeper in the middle. A feeder 2–3m away throws a ball underarm to each cone in turn, allowing the wicketkeeper time to side step across to catch it.

Practice drill for wicketkeeping standing back
Aim: To develop the skill of standing back to seam bowlers.

Equipment: One ball, one set of stumps and one cone per group.

to make them harder or easier, or to train a different element of wicketkeeping.

Wicketkeeping standing back
Description: Wicketkeepers stand back from the stumps when wicketkeeping to fast bowlers and most medium pacers. How far back they stand varies on the speed of the bowler and the pitch, but the ball should reach them at about waist height.

Coaching points:
- Players should start in the basic stance, ensuring they are just to the off side of the stumps with a clear view of the bowler.
- For a straight take, the 'keeper should have their body in line and take the catch with their head over the ball, fingers pointing down (unless it is coming at over waist height).

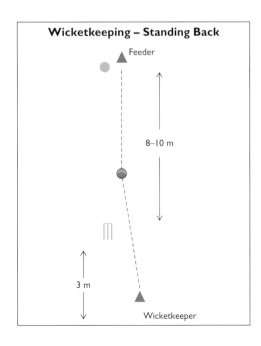

Number of players: Two or three per group.

Explanation: In pairs, one player acting as wicketkeeper takes a basic stance about 3m back from the stumps. The other player stands about 8–10m from the stumps and throws overarm, so that the ball bounces in front of the wickets and reaches the 'keeper at about waist height.

Players have six goes each and then swap. The first six should be straight at the wicketkeeper, the next six to the off side, the next to the leg side, and the last six at random.

Note: This drill can be adapted for standing up to the stumps. Simply move the 'keeper and tell the feeder to throw from a kneeling position with their throwing knee on the floor. For coaching points, see below.

A young wicketkeeper practises the off side take standing up to stumps.

Make it harder: *Throw on to a Katchet board to randomize the feeds. *Vary the speed and bounce of feeds as well as the direction. *Use a smaller ball, for example a child's bouncy ball.

Make it easier: *Tell the feeder to throw underarm from level with the stumps without making the ball bounce. *Tell the player where the feed is going before release. *Remove the stumps.

Wicketkeeping Standing Up

Description: When 'keeping to spinners and slow bowlers, wicketkeepers stand up to the stumps. This ensures that edges will carry, and gives them an opportunity to stump a batsman should they leave the crease.

Leg-side take.

Coaching points: The starting position and main coaching points are similar for standing up as for standing back, but the wicketkeeper may start slightly lower to the ground. It is even more important when standing up that players come up with the ball and don't stand up too soon.

- If off side or down the leg side the wicketkeeper should try to reach the ball by moving their outside leg only, so their inside leg remains close to the stumps. This will keep them in a good position to get a stumping if the chance should arise.
- If the ball bounces below waist height players should move their hands into line by keeping them close to the ground before rising with the ball. This is often called the 'L', as the journey of the hands resembles that letter.
- If the ball bounces above waist height the wicketkeeper should move the leg nearest the ball back on a 45-degree angle and twist their body in the same direction.

Top tip: To help your players test their balance, practise straight takes with a beanbag on their head. If they manage to keep it on, then you know they are keeping their head still and their eyes level throughout the drill.

Practice drill for wicketkeeping standing up

Aim: To develop the skill of taking a stumping when standing up to spinners.

Equipment: One ball, one bat, a set of stumps and one cone per group.

Number of players: Three per group.

Explanation: Set up as for the practice above but with the wicketkeeper standing up

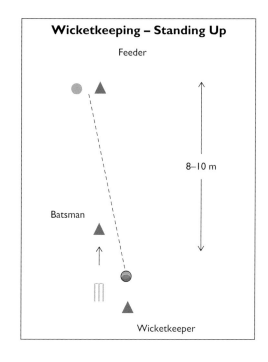

Wicketkeeping – Standing Up

Feeder

8–10 m

Batsman

Wicketkeeper

to the stumps and the feeder kneeling on one knee. Place a player with a bat in front of the stumps.

The feeder throws overarm at random. The batsman's job is to advance down the wicket towards the ball, but to *miss* the ball. The wicketkeeper then takes the ball and tries to remove the bails, as in a stumping.

Make it harder: *Make a game of it so the batter has to advance to a certain point. If they are stumped the 'keeper gets a point, if they get back safely they get a point. *Vary the speed and bounce of feeds as well as the direction. *Use a smaller ball, for example a children's bouncy ball.

Make it easier: *Start without a batsman. *Use an underarm full toss feed. *Tell the batsman to be sure to miss the ball by a long way so the 'keeper's view isn't blocked.

Wicketkeeping catching edges – players need to have quick reactions to catch balls that have been edged behind.

Wicketkeeping Catching Edges

Description: One of the main parts of a wicketkeeper's role is to catch balls that have been edged behind by the batsmen. In order to take these chances, players need to have quick reactions and stay balanced throughout.

Coaching points: The coaching points are the same as for the practices above.

Top tip: Players need to stay low in their stance and come up with the ball. Wicketkeepers also need to ensure they have a clean line of sight to the bowler so they can watch the ball all the way into their gloves.

Practice drill for wicketkeeping catching edges
Aim: To develop the skill of catching balls that have been edged behind.

Equipment: One ball, a set of stumps and two cones per group.

Number of players: Three per group.

Explanation: Like the wicketkeeping practice above, this drill can be set up for both standing up and standing back.

Set up for standing up or standing back, but with a player with a cone in their hand in front of the stumps.

The feeder throws overarm, aiming to get the ball outside off stump and bouncing to about waist height. The player in front of

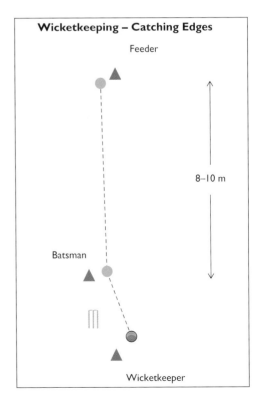

COACHING TECHNIQUE FOR BEGINNERS (UNDER NINES)

Cricket is a highly technical sport and also comes with a whole dictionary full of words that relate to the game but have no meaning in the real world. The combination of these two things can be a barrier to young people trying to learn the game.

While I was working for the Counties Manukau Cricket Association in New Zealand I was lucky enough to work alongside a coach, Peter Zanzottera, who was the best coach of young children (under elevens) that I have had the privilege to work with. Peter had a wonderful manner with the children and made teaching technical skills to youngsters into an art form.

Instead of using complex cricket terms Peter used simple visual images and auditory prompts from everyday life to help children learn new skills. This was incredibly effective, something that became apparent as I visited primary schools where Peter had coached more than a year before. While the children (all of whom were under eleven) may not have been able to remember terms such as 'straight drive', they all recalled the images and prompts that Peter had used with them twelve months earlier.

Below are a few examples. Although it might be slightly outside your comfort zone, I would urge you to try them, or even to come up with your own. As with any normal coaching session with young players, demonstrations are really useful.

High Catch

When introducing the high catch to primary school age pupils, forget complex coaching points and instead ask the children to clap their hands together and open them 'like a book'. When they have done this ask them to spread their fingers out 'to make a bird's nest'. This will give them the basic hand position for the high catch. Finally ask the children to make the sound of a vacuum cleaner as they catch the ball so they are 'sucking the ball' into their nest. This will make them think about 'giving' with their hands and stopping the ball bouncing out of their hands.

Straight Drive

When introducing the concept of the backswing and step for the straight drive, an easy way to get the idea across is to tell your players to think of the pendulum on a grandfather clock. When players swing the bat back they should shout 'tick', and when they bring the bat through to hit the ball they should shout 'tock'. As with a pendulum, the further they swing the bat back, the further they should swing it through – the bigger the 'tick', the bigger the 'tock', and the further the ball will go.

Basic Bowling Action

When introducing the basic bowling action, tell your players to stand with their shoulder (left for right-handers, and vice versa) pointing at their target. Tell them to tie 'an invisible string' between their index fingers on each hand, and start with their non-bowling hand – 'the one without the ball' – pointing up at the sky, and their other hand – 'the one with the ball' – pointing at the ground. Keeping their eyes fixed on the target, the children should pull on the string with their left hand three times (this will bring the left hand down and right hand up). On the third pull they should let go of the ball, bowling it towards their target.

the stumps attempts to make the ball flick the cone on its way through to the wicket-keeper.

If using the drill for standing back you may need to fold the cone in half to make it more rigid, and throw the ball harder to make it reach.

Make it harder: *Vary the speed, bounce and direction of feeds. *Use a smaller ball, such as a children's bouncy ball. *Develop reactions by making the 'keeper start with their back turned and shouting 'turn' just before the player edges the ball.

Make it easier: *Use a sheet of card or paper instead of a cone. *Throw the ball underarm without bouncing. *Use a low compression ball or small football so the feed comes through more slowly.

Team Fielding Drills

As well as developing individual skills, fielding drills can be used to promote important team characteristics. The following practices can improve team work, communication and target setting, and encourage players to evaluate their performance at the same time as honing different fielding techniques. They also offer an element of realism, as players may be required to perform several different skills in a short space of time, much as in a game.

The practices below are suitable for a range of different ages. But as with the majority of drills in this book, you may need to adjust the ball, distances and targets to make it appropriate for your players.

Ground Fielding Triangle
Aim: To develop all the skills needed to field in the ring in a dynamic team practice.

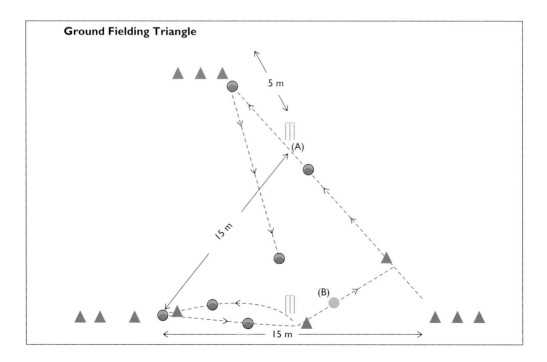

Ground Fielding Triangle

5 m

(A)

15 m

(B)

15 m

Equipment: One ball, two sets of stumps and three cones.

Number of players: Minimum of nine.

Explanation: Mark out a triangle with one set of stumps (a) at the top point and cones as the bottom corners. All should be about 15m apart. Place a second set of stumps (b) between the cones with a wicketkeeper behind them. Place one more cone about 5m back from the top set of stumps (a).

Start with an equal number of players on each cone. The wicketkeeper rolls the ball to group one, who pick up the ball and return it to them using the one-hand pick-up and underarm throw. The wicketkeeper then turns and rolls the ball to group two, who pick the ball up and try to hit the stumps (a) using an overarm throw. Group 3 then collect the ball and throw it back to wicketkeeper, and the practice continues. After fielding the ball, each player 'follows the ball' and joins the group they have just thrown towards.

Make it harder: *Use one stump instead of three. *Tell the wicketkeeper to vary the speed and direction of the feeds. *Introduce a consequence for misfields – for example the whole team does three press-ups.

Make it easier: *Add a second set of stumps for the throwers to aim at. *Decrease the distances between groups and the stumps. *Slow down the speed of feeds from the wicketkeeper.

One-hand Intercept Square

Aim: To develop the one-handed and two-handed intercept and underarm throw in a fast-paced team practice.

Equipment: One ball, one set of stumps and four cones.

Number of players: Minimum of eight.

Explanation: Place four cones in a square about 10 by 10m. Place a set of stumps in the middle, and make sure there are an equal number of players on each cone.

The first player from group A rolls the ball to group B, where the fielder there picks the ball up and throws underarm at the stumps. The first player from group C fields the ball and rolls it to group D. The first player from group D then throws underarm at the stumps. It is fielded by the next player from group A, and the practice continues. After fielding the ball each player 'follows the ball' and joins the group they've just thrown to.

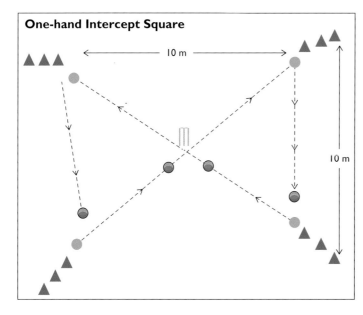

One-hand Intercept Square

10 m

10 m

Make it harder: *Use one stump instead of three. *Tell players to use their weaker hand. *Introduce a second ball starting from group C.

Make it easier: *Use two sets of stumps instead of one. *Make the distance to the stumps smaller. *Slow the feeds and go through at a slow jog/walking pace.

Three-line Catching Challenge

Aim: To develop catching skills in three lines replicating fielding close to the wicket, in the ring and on the boundary.

Equipment: One ball, one set of stumps, one bat or tennis racquet and six cones.

Number of players: Six to twelve (you may need to adjust the cones accordingly).

Explanation: Using cones, create three goals with a gap of 5–10m between each line. The first should be about 5m from the wicketkeeper and about 6m wide; the second should be about 10m wide, and the third about 15m wide. Place equal numbers of players spaced out between each goal.

The coach should stand near the wicketkeeper and hit the ball out at random into the three lines so any player may have to take the catch at a given time. The player takes the catch and returns the ball to the wicketkeeper: the challenge is to take thirty consecutive catches without dropping it. But every ten is a safe number, so for example if

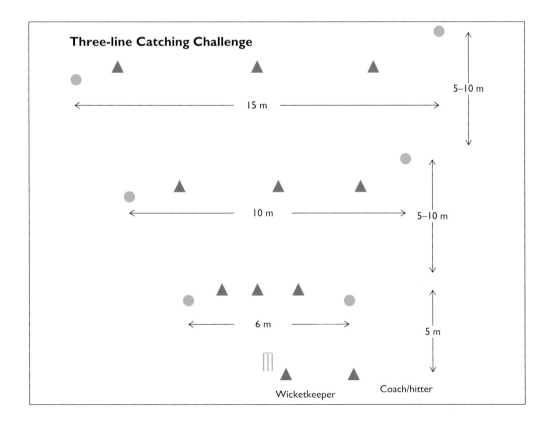

Three-line Catching Challenge

15 m

5–10 m

10 m

5–10 m

6 m

5 m

Wicketkeeper

Coach/hitter

catch nine is dropped, then the team count goes back to 0. If catch twenty-three is dropped the count goes back to the nearest ten, thus twenty in this instance. Players swap lines and positions after each ten. The coach should look to vary the height and speed of catches, as in a game.

Make it harder: *Make the gaps between players bigger. *Increase the 'safe number' to every fifteen catches, or increase the final target number. *Increase the difficulties of the catches.

Make it easier: *Reduce the gaps between players. *The team keeps its score even if they drop the ball. *Hit the ball more slowly and/or nearer to the fielders.

Around the Stumps
Aim: To develop basic fielding skills used in the ring in a realistic team practice.

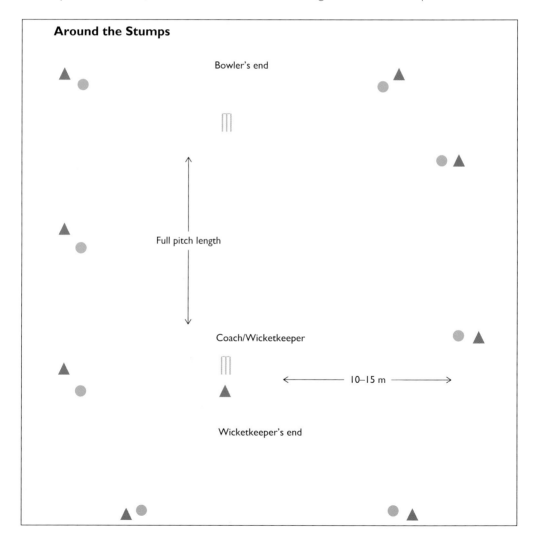

Around the Stumps

Bowler's end

Full pitch length

Coach/Wicketkeeper

10–15 m

Wicketkeeper's end

Equipment: One ball, two sets of stumps and one cone per player.

Number of players: Eight to twelve.

Explanation: Place the stumps a pitch length apart. The coach acting as wicket-keeper should start behind one set of stumps. Around the field place cones in the basic ring fielding positions – cover, point, mid-on, mid-off, midwicket, square leg, short fine leg, short third man – so each player has a cone to stand on.

The coach rolls, throws or hits the ball out wherever they want and shouts either 'bowler's end' or 'keeper's end'. The players must field the ball and throw it to the nominated end. If the call is 'bowler's end' that means a fielder will have to run in to collect the ball there. The coach will then shout a fielding position, and that player has to roll to that fielding position – and the practice continues. Players swap position every six throws.

After a few goes the coach can also introduce the call 'bowler's end shy' or 'keeper's end shy': this means that players must aim for the stumps at the relevant end, and the other fielders must back it up.

Make it harder: *Vary the speed and trajectory of feeds. *Introduce consequences for misfields, such as three press-ups. *Start players with their back to the coach until the ball has been released so they have less time to react.

Make it easier: *Only use the keeper's end. *Limit the feeds to rolling along the floor. *Place an additional set of stumps at each end to increase the target size.

Working in Pairs

Aim: To develop fielding skills used on the boundary while working with a team mate.

Equipment: One ball, two cones, one set of stumps, one bat.

Number of players: Four to twelve.

Explanation: Place two cones about 15m apart and 20–30m away from a single set of stumps. Place a wicketkeeper behind the stumps and two equal groups behind the cones. These fielders should be paired so they are in the opposite group to their partner.

The coach stands near to the wicketkeeper and hits the ball out between the two cones – this can be in the air or along the ground. The pair run out and decide between them who will field the ball. One fielder picks the ball up and the other moves close to them. The player with the ball throws underarm to their partner who then throws it back to the wicketkeeper. The players then join the opposite group from the one they started in.

To make it competitive, award the pair a point for a clean pick-up, a point for a good off-load, and a point for a powerful throw over the top of the stumps. The winning team is the first to gain fifteen points (or whichever score you decide is appropriate for your players).

Make it harder: *Make the gap between the players bigger. *Start players with their back to the coach until the ball has been released so they have less time to react. *Take points off for dropped catches, misfields or poor throws.

Make it easier: *Make the gap between the players smaller. *Bring the players nearer to the stumps. *Hit the feeds nearer to the players or with less power.

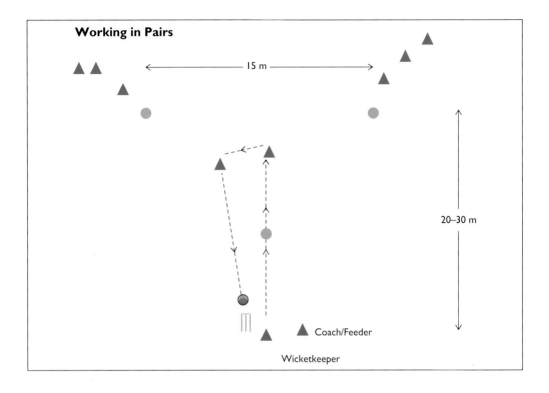

Working in Pairs

15 m

20–30 m

▲ Coach/Feeder

Wicketkeeper

ENCOURAGING SELF-REFLECTION – SCORING OUT OF TEN

Whether you are coaching a technical batting skill in a one-on-one situation or running a team fielding practice, it is important to encourage self-reflection from your players. This gives you a valuable insight into what they are thinking, and helps them to learn more quickly.

One simple way to encourage self-reflection is to ask players to score themselves out of ten during practice sessions. This could be based on their outcome in a particular drill, the amount of effort they are putting in, or how confident they are. The score they give is a useful starting point for follow-up questions. For example, why do you think you are seven? What would the outcome look like if you were a ten? What do we need to do to get there? In team practices the score out of ten can also be applied to the intensity a drill is performed at. For example, if ten is match pace, where are you at the moment as a group?

Remember when using this method that the player's score isn't 'wrong' even if you don't agree with it, as it should be their own, honestly held opinion.

CHAPTER 9

SKILLS, DRILLS AND PRACTICES: GAMES

If you think back to when you or your son/ daughter first learned to play cricket, the chances are that it wasn't through an organized skills practice but through some kind of informal game. In the past cricket may have lost sight of this, but the use of games to teach new skills is now very much an established part of coaching.

The beauty of running a game is that they involve large numbers, are great fun, and provide an opportunity for players to practise a wide range of skills at the same time. The clear benefit of games is that they are as close to a match situation as you can get, and therefore skills learnt in this environment can be easily translated to a competitive one.

Most small-sided games can also be adjusted to place the emphasis on a particular skill or tactical approach. This is often most beneficial when linked to the basic skill session you may have been running earlier. For example, if you have been running a skill practice on playing spin, the game you set up can incorporate this element. Even in something as basic as a non-stop cricket game you can get the bowlers to try spinning the ball, and give the batsmen extra points if they hit with spin.

Games are a great way to end a session, but can be used at any time.

Pairs Cricket
Aim: To develop tactical skills in a match situation.

Equipment: Two sets of stumps, one ball, two bats, and enough cones to mark a boundary.

Number of players: Eight to sixteen.

Explanation: This game can be played between four pairs or two teams. Below is the description for a game where four pairs go head-to-head against each other. If you want to run it as a team game you will follow a similar pattern, but split the group into two teams. The batting team will wait just off the pitch, and the teams will swap after every pair from the batting team has had a go.

Set up a pitch with a set of stumps at each end. Divide players into pairs. Pair one will bat, and they start with twenty runs. The second pair are bowler and wicketkeeper. Pair three starts off fielding on the leg side, and pair four starts on the off side.

The pairs swap after every twelve balls, with the wicketkeeper and bowler swapping after six. Each pair takes it in turn to perform each role. The batsmen try to score as many runs as they can in their two overs. They can be out bowled, caught, run out or hit wicket, and lose five runs each time they are out. The pair with the most runs is the winner.

Ways to adapt the game:

*   Make it hit and run, or remove the boundaries.

Non-stop Cricket

Aim: To develop tactical and technical skills in a fun game situation.

Equipment: One set of stumps, one ball, one bat and three cones.

Number of players: Ten to thirty.

Explanation: Set out a pitch with a bowler about 5m from a set of stumps. Place one cone 5m to the left and another 5m to the right of the stumps. Divide the group into two equal teams, and place the batting team to wait in a safe area about 5m away from the action in line with fine leg.

Each batsman can face a maximum of six balls (this can be less if you have a large group)

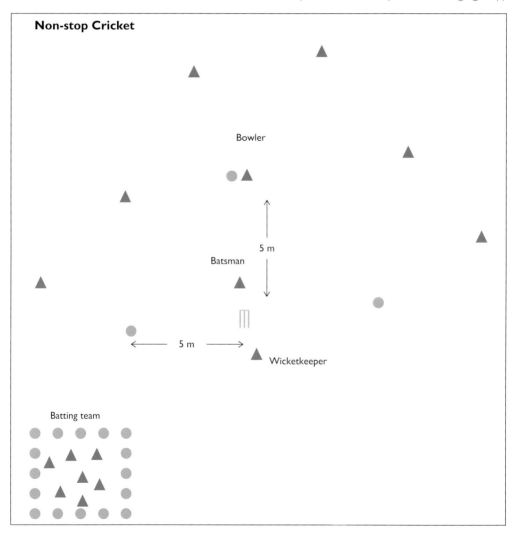

Non-stop Cricket

Bowler

5 m

Batsman

5 m

Wicketkeeper

Batting team

unless they are out before swapping. They score runs by trying to hit the ball, and running around either cone and back to the stumps. They must run every ball, and can run more than once if they choose.

They can be out bowled, caught or hit wicket.

The fielders' job is to collect the ball and return it to the bowler. The bowler delivers the ball underarm, and can bowl as soon as they have the ball even if the batsman is still running. Bowlers swap after six balls each.

After every batsman has batted, the teams swap.

The winning side is the one that scores the most runs.

Ways to adapt the game:

- Introduce 'goals' made with cones in different areas of the field, and introduce bonus runs if the batsmen hit the ball through them. These can be placed at random or in certain areas to promote a certain shot.

Diamond Cricket

Aim: To develop tactical and technical skills in a fun game situation.

Equipment: Four sets of stumps, one ball, four bats and one cone.

Number of players: Sixteen to thirty.

Explanation: Set up a pitch with four sets of stumps 5m apart forming the corners of a square, and all facing inwards.

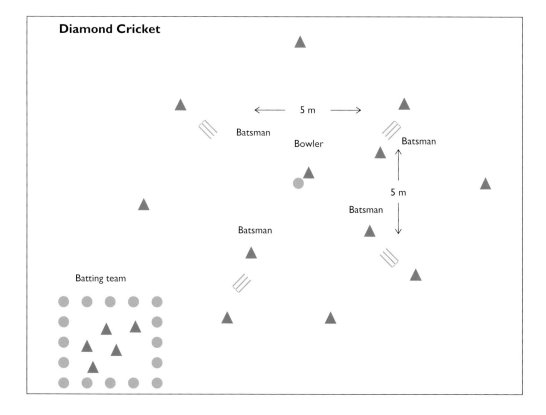
Diamond Cricket

Divide the group into two teams, and place a batsman and wicketkeeper on each set of stumps. You also need a bowler in the centre of the square and fielders around the outside. The remaining batters should wait in a safe area.

The bowler bowls underarm at any batsman they want. A run is scored if every player completes a run anti-clockwise to the next base. A batter can be out bowled, caught or hit wicket, and any batter can be run out at any time.

The bowler and wicketkeepers swap after six balls.

The game can run for a set time period or until all the batters are out. The team with the most runs wins.

Ways to adapt the game:
- Make the batsmen run every ball.
- Introduce boundaries or targets.

Front Foot Drive 'Shoot-out'

Aim: To develop the front foot drive in a competitive game.

Equipment: Two sets of stumps, one ball, one bat and four cones.

Number of players: Eight to sixteen.

Explanation: Place a 'goal' of cones 10–15m in front of a set of stumps. The width of the goal depends on how many fielders you have:

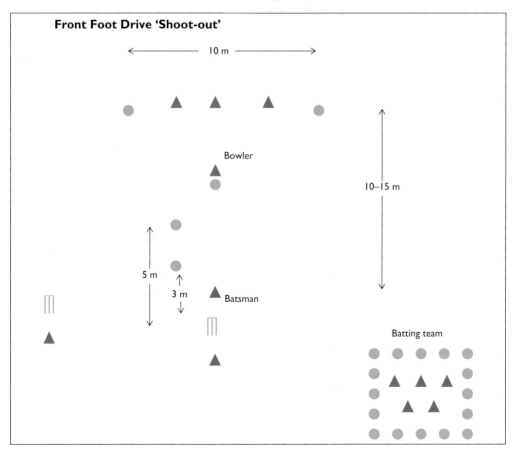

Front Foot Drive 'Shoot-out'

10m is about right for three to four fielders. Place two cones in front of the stumps, one 3m away and the other 5m away. Finally position a wicketkeeper and a second set of stumps level with the batter but 5m to their left.

Divide the group into two teams. The fielding team should have one bowler, one wicketkeeper and the rest of their players in the goal.

Batsmen bat one at a time, and change every six balls unless they are out before that. Bowlers take turns to bowl six balls underarm.

The batsmen get a point for hitting the ball in line with the target, and four for scoring a 'goal'. One bonus point is scored if they also run to the first cone and back, while two are awarded if they make it to the second and get back safely. The fielders must try and stop the ball and return it to the wicketkeeper each time. Batsmen can be out caught, bowled, hit wicket or run out by the wicketkeeper.

Ways to adapt the game:
- Only award points if the ball bounces before reaching the goal.

- Move the goal to encourage different shots (you may also need to adapt the feed).

Pairs Cricket Conditioned Game

Aim: To develop the tactical skill of hitting the gaps.

Equipment: Two sets of stumps, one ball, two bats and enough cones to mark a boundary and six additional boxes.

Number of players: Sixteen to twenty.

Explanation: For this game, set up as you would for a game of pairs cricket between two teams (see above); the only difference is that you also need to create six 'boxes' of cones. These should be about 3 by 3m, with three on the leg side and three on the off side. They can be on any angle, and differing distances from the bat.

As the coach you can condition the game so that the fielding team must have a certain number of players in the boxes at any time. You may decide that every player must be

---

COACHING GAMES

As a coach, games can present a challenge as they are fast paced and there is a lot going on at once. This can make observations difficult, and it can be a problem to stop the game for fear of interrupting its natural flow. Therefore you are left with two choices of how to run a game. One is to take a step back and let the game unfold, where your role is to observe the play and note down strengths and areas to improve to discuss with your players at the end of an innings or the match. This allows the game to flow, but has the disadvantage that any intervention may come too late for players to put your advice into practice. It is also easy to forget what you have seen!

The other way is to move around during the game and ask questions of specific players or groups of players at appropriate times. This questioning style has the advantage of giving individuals the chance to use their learning to influence the game straightaway. However, it can also distract them and interrupt the practice.

These styles are both useful in their own way, and as with the coaching tools described in Chapter 2, the best coaches will become comfortable with both and will use them as they think appropriate to best support their players.

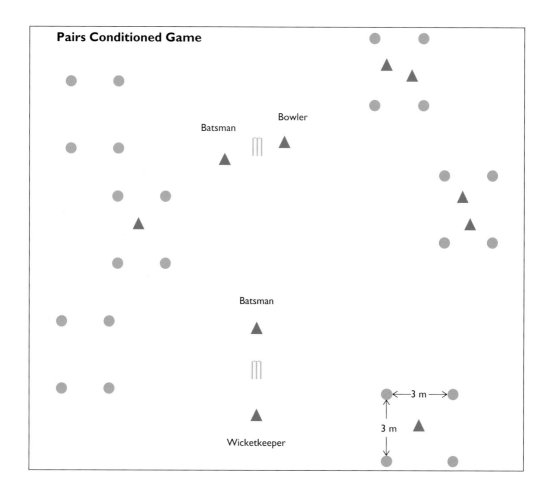

Pairs Conditioned Game

in the same box, or simply leave it open by saying that two fielders must be in a box and let the fielding team decide which one.

The idea is that you encourage batsmen to think about where they hit the ball – for example, where there are no fielders – and that bowlers adjust their lines to stop them doing it.

There are countless different combinations, but always think about what you are trying to encourage your players to do.

Ways to adapt the game:
• Make it hit and run.
• Remove the boundaries.

CHAPTER 10

SKILLS, DRILLS AND PRACTICES: NETS

Nets are one of the most valuable yet misused resources available to a coach – especially as your players get older and more experienced. They are valuable because they can provide good quality practice in a safe and confined area. They are misused because too often players simply 'have a net'. In my experience when most players are told to 'have a net' all focus and discipline disappears and the session breaks down. Because they are relatively easy to manage they can also become a coach's sole method of training, which means the players will not develop into well rounded cricketers.

This section provides some ideas on how to gain maximum value from a net practice. Below are a few tips to help get you started.

Limit the number of players: Club nets are often used as crowd control rather than as a tool for quality practice. Limit numbers to a maximum of eight per net: one batsman, a second padding up, and six bowlers.

Have a focus: Nets work best when the practice has a specific focus. This might be, for example, setting up a match scenario – maybe the first ten overs of a match, working on a technical development such as hitting the ball with the full face of the bat, or a tactical move, such as bowlers focusing on trying to hit a certain line and length.

Have consequences: Often discipline breaks down in a net because the batsman knows they have ten minutes to bat regardless of how many times they are out. Try running sessions in which when players are out, that is the end of their net, or in which bowlers have to do a mild forfeit if they bowl wides, for example three press-ups/sit-ups.

Don't go on for too long: As with all practices, a net session is better done for a short time at a high intensity than for a long time at a lower rate.

Top Five Nets

When You Are Out, You're Out

Aim: To replicate some of the pressures of a match in a net practice.

Equipment: A net, two sets of stumps, one ball per bowler.

Number of players: One batsman batting, a second padded up waiting to bat, and up to six bowlers.

Explanation: In a net practice there is typically no consequence for batsmen when they are out. To replicate the pressures of a game, enforce a 'when you are out you are out' rule. This simply means that if a player is dismissed in a net that is the end of their innings and they are replaced by another batsman.

To add extra realism, tell the bowlers to place cones in the net to replicate field settings. Red cones on the ground denote close fielders and yellow denote ring fielders. To mark boundary fielders, fold a cone in half and thread it through the netting: if the ball goes in the air near one of these 'fielders', that counts as a player being caught out.

The decisions should be made by an umpire. This could be the bowler who bowled the previous ball, the waiting batsman, or the coach.

Ways to adapt the net:
- Allow batsmen five minutes to 'play themselves in' before enforcing the rules.
- Allow the player two lives before they are given out caught.
- Tell bowlers to bowl three consecutive balls each.

Match Scenarios: Opening Up

Aim: To replicate the opening phase of an innings in a net practice.

Equipment: A net, two sets of stumps, one new ball per bowler.

Number of players: Two batsmen batting, two bowlers.

Explanation: One of the most crucial phases of any match is the opening overs. In order to prepare for this effectively you should try to ensure that the conditions in a net practice are as close to the real thing as they can be. Therefore you need to make sure your opening batsmen face your opening bowlers, and the bowlers are armed with a new ball. As in the previous net practice, the bowlers should mark their fields with cones. Make sure these are realistic – for example, fields should be attacking with close catchers, and few, if any, men on the boundary.

The bowlers should bowl in four-ball overs with the batsmen swapping ends after every

three balls, or when they think there is a single available. This will help them switch their concentration on and off, as in a match.

Before starting, agree a target for the batsmen – for example, 30–0 in fourteen four-ball overs. The coach or the player who has just bowled should stand in the umpire's position and score the practice to ensure that it is as realistic as possible.

Ways to adapt the net:
- Bring in consequences if targets aren't reached – for example, the 'winning' pair can decide a small forfeit for the losers, such as twenty press-ups.
- Introduce 'when you are out you are out', and have other batsmen ready to come in.
- Use one batsman.

Match Scenarios: the Middle of an Innings

Aim: To replicate the middle phase of an innings in a net practice.

Equipment: A net, two sets of stumps, one ball per bowler.

Number of players: Two batsmen batting, or one batting and one padded up; three to six bowlers (a mixture of both seam and spin).

Explanation: During the middle overs of a match the field typically will become more spread as batsmen start to try and increase the run rate. Set up a net as before, but this time instead of marking the field with cones, mark the gaps: like this it will be easy for the batsmen to see what their most productive scoring areas are likely to be. Thus red cones denote a gap through which a boundary can be scored, while yellow show a gap where a single or hard-run two may be available.

As with the other net practices, this can be done with one batsmen or two changing ends every few balls. It can be done with bowlers bowling four-ball overs, or with four to six bowlers taking it in turns. The key thing is that an appropriate target is set for the batsmen, and this is scored by the bowlers, coach or a waiting batsman. This target should be higher than for opening the innings – for example, at a rate of between four and five runs per over.

Ways to adapt the net:
- Bring in consequences if targets aren't reached – for example, the 'winning' pair can decide a small forfeit for the losers, such as twenty press-ups.
- Introduce 'when you are out you are out', and have other batsmen ready to come in.
- Use spinners instead of seam bowlers.

Match Scenarios: the End of an Innings

Aim: To replicate the end of a one-day innings in a net practice.

Equipment: A net, two sets of stumps, one ball per bowler.

Number of players: One batsman, three to six bowlers.

Explanation: This net practice should replicate the end of an innings when batsmen are looking to attack and score runs at a high rate. For this situation have one batsman and three to six bowlers taking it in turn to bowl. Although it is not the same as in a match,´

facing different bowlers each ball is useful for the batsman in this instance as it is similar to the end of a match when a single bowler may bowl a number of variations. Although you may decide to introduce consequences if the batsman gets out, I would not advise 'when you are out you're out' as you don't want to deter the batsman from experimenting and attacking as much as possible. Instead you might give them a certain number of 'lives'.

Set up a net as above, marking the gaps with cones. As with the other practices it is crucial that an appropriate target is set for the batsmen, and this is scored by the bowlers, coach or a waiting batsman. This target should be higher than for the middle of the innings – for example, at a rate of six runs per over or more.

Ways to adapt the net:
- Introduce a number of 'lives' for the batsman.
- Introduce consequences if the bowlers bowl wides or no balls – for example, three press-ups.

Physical Net

Aim: To develop fitness and concentration when fatigued in a net practice.

Equipment: A net, two sets of stumps, one ball per bowler.

Number of players: One batsman, two or three bowlers.

MIDDLE PRACTICES

If you do not have a net facility, or if you want to make your tactical sessions more match-like, then all the ideas in this section can be used out in the middle instead. This has the added benefit of allowing you to use fielders (instead of cones), which increases the number of people involved and the realism of the situation.

Explanation: As well as developing tactical and technical skills, nets can also be used to improve fitness. Set up as for a normal net, but the bowlers bowl in three-ball overs, sprinting to the end of their run-up after each ball. The batsman has to sprint a two after every three balls. If you have a third bowler, set up so that one player is bowling, the player that has just bowled is resting, and the one about to bowl is performing another exercise – for example, squats while they are waiting.

Ways to adapt the net:
- Make the batsmen run fours.
- Give the waiting bowler other exercises – for example press-ups, sit-ups, bowling a heavy ball to a partner such as a basketball or medicine ball.

FITNESS

It is important that the fitness elements you choose are not too strenuous, and that the practice doesn't go on too long, particularly if working with young players. If you notice bowlers' actions breaking down or batsmen looking too tired, then you should stop. For under-thirteen players, this practice should serve more as a way to improve their concentration as they become tired, than a way to improve fitness.

CHAPTER 11

SESSION PLANNING AND DIFFERENTIATION

Whether you prefer to use an iPad or draw diagrams on scrap paper, there is no one 'right' way to plan a coaching session – the important thing is simply that you take the time to do it. A number of session-planning templates are available online, and the ECB's Howzat computer program (available to ECBCA members) is also an excellent resource. But the key is to find a method of planning that suits you and is clear and simple to follow.

Session Planning

As all coaches are unique, the way they run their sessions will be subtly different. There should also be room for coaches to be intuitive, and to change their plans as they go along. But for the purposes of this book we will look at the elements that are common to good sessions and good session planning.

Structure and allocating time

There are many different ways to structure a coaching session, but the outline below is an example of an effective way to divide your time when working with a typical under-eleven group over a 90min training night.

- Warm-up: 0–15min
- Skill practice: 15–40min
- Short break: 45–50min
- Game or net session: 50–80min
- Reflections and cool down: 80–90min

Players

As discussed earlier in the book, our goal is to deliver coaching sessions that are built around the specific needs of our players. Identifying what you want your players to achieve is an excellent way to start planning your session. Once you have worked out what your players' learning objective is, it will be much easier to decide on the types of practice methods you use, and the different technical, tactical, physical and mental factors you want to cover.

When planning for the session it is useful to ask yourself the following questions:

- Who are my players? (Age and so on)
- How many are there?
- What is their current experience/skill level?
- What do they need to work on? (These could be technical, tactical, physical or mental aspects)
- What outcome do I want to help them achieve?

Space and equipment

One of the key things to consider when planning a coaching session is the space you are working in, and the equipment you have available. When planning the session, think about the following points:

- How much space do I have available?
- What is the ground/floor surface like?
- What equipment, and how much of it do I have available?

- Is the equipment appropriate for my players?
- What are the main safety considerations?

Practices

Once you have considered your players and the environment you are coaching in, you will be able to decide on the exact practices you will run in your coaching session. At all times you need to ensure the following:

- The practice must be safe.
- It should be appropriate for the skill level of the players, and cover what they need to learn.
- The maximum number of players should be involved at all times, and everyone should have equal opportunities.
- The practices should be simple to set up and easy to explain.
- There must be opportunities for players to learn new skills and/or gain new information.
- Appropriate progressions should be offered during the session.
- A high rate of activity should be maintained, without dwelling on the same thing for too long.

Coaching tools

The final thing to consider when planning your session is your role as a coach and the coaching tools you will use. Although some of this is likely to change based on what you observe in your session, it is still worth considering some of the following things beforehand:

- Do I understand my practices sufficiently to give a clear, concise explanation?
- Will I use a demonstration? If so when will I use it? Will I do it myself, use a player, another coach or a video?

- What will my main coaching points be for each section of the practice, and how will I get these across? For example instructions, questions, demonstration
- What will I need to observe during the session?
- How will I make the session harder/easier if required?

Cool-downs and reflections

Even though children generally don't need a cool-down for the same physical reasons as adults, this is still an important part of the session. The cool-down is a chance to get your players to calm down after activity, to rehydrate, and to reflect on the session they have just done.

With time at a premium it is always tempting to miss out this part of the session, but it is an excellent way to reinforce the learning that has gone on, and to give players something to look forward to for the following week. Like a warm-up, there is a wide range of things you could do in a cool-down. The most important of these include:

- Reducing the heart rate and bringing the body back to a resting state
- Reinforcing the key learning from the session through questions
- Highlighting what has gone well during the session, and telling the players what will happen in the following week
- Rehydrating – having a drink

A cool-down and reflection session generally only needs to take 5–10min. Depending on the age of your group you could also do a few static stretches to improve flexibility and reduce stiffness in the muscles. Although most under-thirteens won't need this, it is no bad thing to get them into a good habit, which will serve them well as they get older.

Differentiation

Differentiation in a cricket setting is simply the ability to adapt your coaching sessions to different individuals. Although a simple concept, it can often be quite a challenge in a typical club session where your players may range from beginners to county age-group players.

As already discussed earlier, the ability to deliver player-centred coaching sessions that cater for the needs of everyone in your group is central to good coaching. Any drill or practice can be adapted in any number of ways to make it harder or easier as required. The same principles can also be used when working with players with a disability.

When attempting to use differentiation, you may consider simply splitting your group in ability and running two separate variations of the practice side by side, one for the better players and the other for the weaker ones. However, the problem with this plan is that the players in the weaker group may feel unhappy that they have been categorized in this way; it can also create a divide between the two sets of players. The real challenge of using differentiation well is to incorporate the different adaptations in one single session that involves everyone. The best way to do this is to provide different levels of challenge but leave the choice of which one they choose down to the player themselves.

An example of this is the conditioned non-stop cricket game described in Chapter 9. There the coach adjusts the rules, scoring and equipment to cater for different abilities. In doing this he weights the game so there is a greater reward for those taking a higher risk, or choosing to challenge themselves. What you will usually find is that your players will choose a level of challenge that is appropriate to them, because we all want to achieve success. The crucial thing here is that it is the players that choose their level of challenge, and not the coach, therefore any stigma is taken away. Keep this in mind when thinking of how to implement differentiation in your sessions.

In a typical practice there are five areas that can be altered to cater for different levels of ability: equipment, space, feeds, scoring/targets, and rules.

Equipment

By changing the equipment used you can increase or decrease the challenge of a practice. Thus, if you are running a batting drill you can make the practice harder by using a stump or sawn down 'middle bat'; with beginners or someone with a disability you can make it easier by using a tennis racquet.

Another piece of equipment you can change is the ball. A bigger ball is easier in catching and hitting practice, whereas a golf ball, squash ball or reaction ball can make it harder.

Space

Depending on the type of practice you are running, making the space bigger or smaller can influence the difficulty level. In a game of non-stop cricket, the further the batter has to run, the harder the drill. The same is true if you increase the height of a high catch, or place players further from the target in an overarm throw practice.

However, if a player is taking part in a batting or wicketkeeping drill for example, decreasing the distance will increase the difficulty as their reaction time will be lowered.

Feeds

The type of feed will have a strong bearing on the difficulty of fielding and batting practices. To increase the challenge, make the feeds faster and more variable; to make them easier, slow feeds down and make them more predictable. For example, if you are running a close catching drill, the practice will be much easier if the player knows that the ball will come at the same (slow) speed, height and direction every time. If the feed varies in height and direction at random and at a fast pace, then it becomes much more difficult.

To reduce a drill to its simplest level you can use a static ball. This could be used to help players master the one-handed pick-up, or could involve batters hitting off a tee.

Feeds are particularly important in batting practices. For front shots the general progression is from a tee to a drop feed, to a bobble feed, to an underarm throw, and finally to a full overarm feed. For back foot shots start with a tee, then move to a full toss thrown underarm from the point where the ball would have bounced. From there you can then move back to a full overarm feed.

Full details of feeding for batting can be found in Chapter 6, in the section 'Feeding for Batting'.

Scoring/targets

An easy way to adjust the difficulty of a practice is to adjust the size of a target. Increasing the size of a scoring area in batting, bowling or fielding will make the drill easier, whereas decreasing it will make it harder. For example in a bowling drill such as the one described in Chapter 7 'Target Bowling'/'Bowl Off', you can adjust the number of stumps the bowler has to aim at. With beginners you might start with three sets of wickets side by side, but for experienced players you could start with a single stump.

You can also tweak the method of scoring to differentiate the practice. For example, you might make a batting practice harder by limiting the batsman to only scoring on the off side, whereas to make it easier you might offer shorter boundaries. Another method would be to offer multiple scoring zones, but incentivize them so the one that is hardest to score in is worth the most points.

Rules

Making changes to the rules of a game or drill can have a big effect on the difficulty of the practice. For example, in a conditioned game you may tell players they have to run every ball, or they are out if they play and miss three times. Going the other way, you may say batsmen can't be out first ball, or will receive double runs for using a certain shot – for example, front foot drive.

CHAPTER 12

RUNNING A TEAM

Although a large part of this book focuses on helping you run dynamic, player-centred coaching sessions, the role of a coach is not confined to what you do on training nights: as a club or school coach you are also likely to be responsible for managing a team through the season. This comes with a number of different challenges to those you face in your coaching sessions. From helping your players apply their skills in a competitive match, to team selection and dealing with parents, you will need to consider a number of additional areas. Below are a few ideas on how to approach a number of the common issues and questions that you may face as the coach of a team.

Development versus Winning

A life of frustration is inevitable for any coach whose main enjoyment is winning.
Chuck Noll (Steelers Coach)

There is no question that winning is a good thing. Winning gives your players a good feeling and is a clear measure of successful performance. But should winning be a team's sole focus or the only measure of success?

If you were coach of the England senior team then the answer to this may well be yes. But as the coach of a club or school youth team the conclusion should be very different – especially in the younger age groups. As a junior coach your job is simply to help your players learn and enjoy the game of cricket.

And while winning matches may contribute to both of these, there are other things you need to consider.

Just as you plan your coaching sessions to ensure that everyone is involved, you also need to think about this in relation to matches. If you are winning matches but only a handful of players are being given the opportunity to contribute, then those who are not involved will become unhappy and disillusioned with the game. This could cause them to feel resentment towards you and the other players, and it could cause them to give up playing altogether. Is this success?

As mentioned earlier in the book, young players develop at different rates, and your best players at nine years old may not still be your best players at seventeen. And perhaps more pertinently, there may be apparently mediocre players in your under-eleven team who will not start to show their true potential until much later. Identifying which players this applies to is impossible. However, one thing that is certain is that if you do not afford them the opportunities to keep improving, then they never will.

If winning is your sole focus at under eleven you may well win the league, but you will be in danger of finding that by the time your players reach under seventeen and senior cricket, only a handful will have achieved their potential, or are still playing. If you choose development over winning you should accept that it is unlikely that your younger age groups will win silverware. However, by giving these youngsters opportunities at under nine, eleven and thirteen, there is a strong chance that they will be a force to be reckoned with as they get older – something that most people would agree is a much more important outcome.

The challenge for you as a coach is that while winning versus developing players is not a straight choice, it is at the very least a skilled balancing act. While you want to reward successful performance, you should never lose sight of the need to keep developing all your players, no matter what their rate of development might be.

Team selection and player roles

To develop your players not only do you need to ensure they are all given opportunities to play, they also need to perform in a number of different roles. In younger age groups this means giving players the chance to bat, bowl and field in different positions, and to give more than one player the chance to keep wicket.

As well as ensuring that everyone is involved, this approach allows them to experience what is required of them in different match situations. For example, while moving someone from opening the batting to number six could be viewed as a demotion, it should be viewed as an opportunity for them to learn a different role. It is also beneficial for a number of players to have the opportunity to be captain. This improves their understanding of the game, and helps you create a whole team of 'thinking cricketers'.

While there is no problem with rewarding successful performance, never lose sight of the long-term aim of producing a whole squad of well rounded players. Specialization can come later.

Parents

The support of parents is critical to running a successful youth team, but it isn't always a straightforward relationship. The vast majority will be more than happy to assist you in any way they can, from making teas to helping with lifts to matches. But because parents' priority is their son or daughter, this may at times create conflict with what you are trying to do from a team perspective.

One of the problems you may encounter when taking a 'development first' approach is that you will almost certainly face questions over your decisions. For example, a parent may want to know why their son opened bowling last week but didn't come on until second change today. As coach you should be prepared to explain your thinking, and to take time to ensure that parents, players and fellow coaches understand your rationale.

One way of doing this is to hold a parents' meeting prior to the season so that you can give them an insight into your plans, and they can ask any questions they might have. It may also be useful to think about the roles of your players for a few games at a time, and share this with parents so that they get an idea of your medium-term plans.

Some clubs get their parents to sign up to a code of conduct outlining their role and what is expected of them during a season. I have never found this necessary, and believe that clear, regular communication is the key to a happy coach/parent relationship.

Player discipline

One of the subjects that often comes up between coaches of young players is how to deal with difficult behaviour. A lack of discipline can undermine the coach, disrupt a coaching session, diminish the experience for the other players and jeopardize safety. Although there is no single magic solution to prevent this happening, you can do a number of things that minimize the incidence and effects of bad behaviour:

Know your players

As with other areas of your coaching, knowing your players is crucial in preventing challenging behaviour. As you get to know them you will be able to identify which players may need extra attention, and will begin to understand what it is that causes them to behave badly. Do they come straight from school and are tired? Do they get bored easily? Are there certain other players they don't get on with? Do they struggle to control their emotions in a competitive situation?

Once you know which players are more likely to behave badly, and why this is, you can plan accordingly. For example there may be certain players you don't want to work together, some players need more encouragement than others, and some may simply need regular drinks breaks or 'time out' periods.

Equally, while you look to eradicate bad behaviour, don't forget to praise good behaviour where appropriate. A good way to develop positive behaviour, even with very young players, is to hand over some responsibility to them. Asking them questions, getting them to make decisions about their practice sessions, and discussing what it means to be a good team-mate, can all be useful.

Coach behaviour

As a coach you are a role model to the children you coach and your behaviour will set the tone for the session. If you aren't punctual, polite and wear suitable attire, it is unreasonable to expect it from your players. It is important to make eye contact with your players and to address them both as a group and as individuals. Using regular praise, and being consistent in your manner and the standards you set will all help build a positive relationship with your players.

The practice

One of the main reasons for difficult behaviour is boredom. In a way this is good news for coaches as it is something that we can directly influence. By making sure players are active quickly, that everyone is involved, and sessions move at a fast pace, you can ensure that your group is engaged throughout.

It is also important that the level of the challenges you set is appropriate for your players. Too easy and they quickly become bored, two hard and they may become frustrated and disillusioned. Both instances are likely to lead to a break down in behaviour.

When planning your sessions try to think of something new to do with your players each week. Although some repetition may be necessary to reinforce learning, try to do something different with your players every time you see them. This will keep them on their toes and ensure that sessions remain fresh over the course of a long season.

Finally, consider the equipment you use. The kit you incorporate into your drills needs to be appropriate for the stage of player you are coaching – for example, under-thirteens will become annoyed if they are only working with tennis balls and plastic bats. Equally, if you use cricket balls with seven-year-olds who have never played before then you are compromising their safety and as a result their behaviour will break down.

Code of behaviour

Although there is plenty you can do to help prevent difficult behaviour, it is impossible to eradicate it completely. To make sure you are supported as a coach your club should have some kind of club-wide code of behaviour and disciplinary procedure in place. Ideally this should be something that a player's parents sign up to on their behalf detailing what is expected from them and what the consequences will be if they don't comply.

If your club doesn't have something like this, then the best place to go for guidance is your local school. Schools will all have set procedures for dealing with bad behaviour, which can easily be incorporated by your club. For example, some have a yellow and red card system, as in football. In this instance a child will receive a warning the first time they step out of line, and some kind of punishment if they do it again. Schools will also have systems in place for rewarding good behaviour – these are also worth using in your sessions.

Whatever system you decide upon, the important thing is that it is implemented across the club and that parents are fully aware of it, so that should you need to take action you are fully supported.

Coaching on Match Days

As coaches, everything we do is built around helping our players to perform in matches. But what exactly is our role before, during, and after the game?

Pre-match
As coach of a club or school, your role will start long before the first ball is bowled. From getting players to the game, organizing umpires, making sure you have a pitch, finding a scorebook and ensuring you have match balls, there is a lot to plan in advance. If you are lucky you may have a manager to assist you with this, but the reality is that at most clubs you will have to be responsible for most of the administration prior to a game. On the day of the match your focus should be on your team and helping them to be successful on the pitch.

The warm-up
How long this takes and what this entails will depend on the amount of time you have available and the age of the players you are working with. Remember that this should not be an extra training session – it is simply about preparing players for the match ahead. This means making sure their bodies are warmed up physically, and that they are starting to think about the game ahead from a tactical point of view. For an under-nine team playing after school, half an hour to get changed and go through one or two simple, fun practices – for example, a game of hand hockey or a simple fielding drill – to get your players thinking about cricket should be ample.

For an under-thirteen team playing a thirty-five-over match on a Sunday I would advise getting your players on the field to warm-up around an hour before the start of play.

Below is an example of a typical warm-up for the scenario above. To make it applicable to your age group or situation simply scale the times down and change the practices as required.

0–10min: Game of hand hockey or similar.

10–20min: Dynamic stretches and a short team talk to discuss the match ahead – for example, the pitch, conditions, opposition and tactics. This talk should be facilitated by the coach but led by the players. It may also include looking at the pitch and deciding whether you should bat or bowl first.

20–30min: Team fielding drill, such as 'Team Fielding Triangle'.

30min from the start: Try to get your captain to do the toss so you know whether you will be batting or bowling.

40–45min: This is a chance for the bowlers to bowl, for example, Target Bowling (Chapter 7), and for the batsmen to hit some throw-downs (see text box). Players do not need to be out there for the whole fifteen minutes – especially the bowlers – but this time is allowed so that all-rounders have a chance to both bat and bowl.

This period also affords you the opportunity to talk to the individual members of your team. For example, you may want to talk to your batsmen about the batting order, or discuss field settings with your bowlers.

45–50min: Players have a drink and get changed.

50–55min: Final team chat. This would typically be on setting targets for the game – for example, what do we want the score to be after fifteen overs, and how are we going to do it? It is also a chance to answer any last questions the players may have.

55–60min: Leave the players to get ready.

During the match

For many coaches the hours of play can be both the most rewarding and the most frustrating part of your role. On a good day you may be able to sit back and watch your players put into practice everything they have learned during your coaching sessions. But on other occasions you may be left watching powerless from the side as your team makes a series of basic mistakes. Frustrating though this is, it is part and parcel of coaching a junior team – or

---

THROW-DOWNS

'Throw-downs' is the term used to describe a simple batting practice where a batsman hits balls thrown by a feeder. They are commonly used before a match to help batsmen prepare for the game ahead. Used well they can improve confidence and get the batsmen used to watching the ball, hitting it in the middle of the bat, and moving their feet. But unfortunately they are often misused, which can have a negative impact on a player's preparation. Below are a few tips for throw-downs prior to a match:

Find a suitable place to practise: When doing throw-downs you need a secure area for the batsmen to hit into, such as netting, or a secure fence. Ideally, throw-downs should also be practised on a good surface such as a net or practice wicket.

Make sure they have a focus: Simply having throw-downs for the sake of it can be a waste of time, so make sure your players know what they want to achieve: for example, hitting a certain number of balls in the middle of the bat on the front foot, and a set number on the back foot.

Make sure the feed is appropriate: Just like any other batting practice, it is crucial that if throw-downs are to be worthwhile, the feed is appropriate. The type of feed will depend on what shot the batsman wants to play, and what surface you are practising on. For example, if you have a good surface – such as a net or artificial wicket – you can throw overarm and allow the ball to bounce. But if there is no suitable surface available you are much better off throwing full tosses. All too often I have had to stop practices because throw-downs are taking place on a bumpy patch of outfield. This results in uneven bounce and is detrimental for the batsman.

It is also important to ensure the feeder is an appropriate distance from the batsman, and again, this will depend on the type of feed. The feeder needs to be far enough away for the batsman to have time to react, but close enough to make sure their feed is accurate.

any team for that matter. However much we may want to step in, it is important to resist the temptation and to give your players the freedom to learn the game for themselves – including allowing them to make mistakes.

If you step in every time you see something going wrong the players will never learn for themselves. Shouting and gesticulating from the sidelines is also questionable sportsmanship – the match is between the teams, not the coaches – and can disrupt the game.

I was once coaching a district under-fifteen team at a ground with a quick pitch and short, straight boundaries. Despite talking about field settings before the game, we started without a third man and almost immediately began conceding runs through this area as the opposition got off to a flyer. Walking around the boundary in the opening few overs I was sorely tempted to have a word with the man at fine leg on my way past, but decided I would wait and see how long it took them to react.

The answer proved to be eleven overs and around sixty runs – at least half of these through third man. Although it was frustrating to watch and put us at a disadvantage in the game, I was actually pleased with what had happened. Yes, it had taken much longer for the captain and bowler to react, but the important thing was that eventually they did – and without any interference from me. Later we discussed why it had taken so long, and what the impact on the game had been, but the experience proved to be a lesson learned as it didn't happen again that season.

While it is important as a coach not to get involved in the match, there are a number of things that you can do during a game to support your team and help them keep learning.

When your team is batting

Even when coaching a young team it is always a good idea to make sure the team sits together during their innings. Not only does this mean they are more likely to watch the game, but it can build team spirit and gives you the chance to discuss the match situation with your players.

At the start of an innings tell your players to set up a 'base camp' with a few chairs or benches, and designate this as your team area. It is helpful if this area is near the scorers or at least in view of the scoreboard. During the innings you can question your players on a number of different areas, from target setting, to the best run-scoring areas, and what they have noticed about certain bowlers. Sometimes it can be good to set these questions to the whole team, but often it can be better to do this individually or in small groups. At all times your team should be aware of the score and their targets, whether this is in a run chase or setting a total.

As a coach you shouldn't communicate directly with the batsmen on the field of play unless in a designated drinks break (with the permission of the umpires and opposition). Instead you should limit your influence to sending out a simple message with an incoming batsman if required.

It is up to you to decide whether you allow players to visit their parents or go to the nets during a match, but it is important that if they are under eleven they should be supervised at all times. I will generally allow young players the chance to visit their parents briefly to collect a drink or some sun cream, but I try to keep the group together. I also do not encourage practice during the game as it is not usually beneficial and can often prove a distraction.

When your team is fielding

When your team is in the field it is a case of handing over to them. Discussions on field settings and bowling plans should have been done beforehand, and in a match it is up to your players to put these into practice. Nevertheless although you are not actively involved in the match, your job as a coach is far from over.

While your team is on the field your role is to observe the action and note – either physically or mentally – anything that you think will be useful to bring up in your post-match debrief. These should be both things your team is doing well and areas to improve. They could be technical aspects such as an excellent throw or a failure to get into the ready position in the field, or they could be tactical things such as field placings.

Just as you would when observing players in practice sessions, try to move around the boundary to watch the action from different places. To observe bowlers, the best positions are from behind the wicketkeeper or from the bowler's end, ensuring you are not behind the bowler's arm.

Although it is acceptable to have a quiet word with a boundary fielder on the way past, you should avoid communicating with your players until a drinks break. As long as it has been agreed with the umpires and opposition in advance, this is an opportunity to talk to your players and ask them what their thoughts are on the game. While you are free to offer suggestions, this chat should be led by the players with you asking questions to stimulate their tactical thinking.

If you do not have a twelfth man, then another part of your role may be to make sure your bowlers have drinks available at fine leg, and that any protective equipment, such as a wicketkeeper's helmet, is available if required.

Post match

Often the end of a match results in a frantic rush to pack up kit and head home, but the time directly after the end of play is a vital part of your young players' cricketing education. It is an opportunity to reflect on the game, reinforce the positives, and discuss any areas that may need improvement. These sessions don't need to take any more than ten minutes, but it is important that your players – and their parents – understand that they are a crucial part of the match day.

If you have time they can include a few cool-down exercises, but the most important part is the chat with your players. While your input is valuable, your aim should be to draw out through questioning the main points you have observed. During this time you should encourage players to talk about what they have done well, and to give examples. You should also pick out any areas to improve, and what they might do differently next time. It is useful to have the scorebook to hand at this stage in order to back up any points that are made. Try to ask questions to both the group and individuals so that everyone is involved in the discussion.

Your skill as a coach will then be to take all the views and information that your players have come up with, and going forwards, to consolidate this into two or three things to focus on. These should be both positives and areas to improve.

CHAPTER 13

EXTRAS

What Next?

For coaches in any sport it is important to keep learning and developing, both for your own benefit and that of your players. A coach who feels they know it all has usually become stale and will struggle to inspire their team. Although some elements of cricket have remained the same for more than a hundred years, the game is always evolving and it is vital that as a coach you match this evolution.

To continue your development and keep your ideas fresh there are a number of things you can do, including self reflection, observing other coaches, and attending a coaching course or workshop.

Self reflection

The simplest and most powerful tool to help you develop as a coach is to continually reflect on your coaching sessions. Sometimes a practice will run perfectly, while at other times you will notice a number of ways to improve it. This happens at all levels and is all a part of coaching. No one runs successful sessions every single time – the important thing is to review and refine them as necessary.

Your reflections can be written down, typed up, discussed with a fellow coach, or thought about in the car as you drive home from practice. There is no right way to reflect – the important thing is that you take the time to do so.

Finally, don't forget to reflect on the positive and successful aspects of your sessions.

What you have done well is just as important as the things you need to improve.

Observe other coaches

As I may have mentioned earlier in the book, the best coaches I know are unashamed thieves. If you see another coach doing something well, you should have no qualms about trying it in your own sessions. That is not to say that you should copy it exactly – it is always good to put your own slant on things – but watching and learning from other coaches will be a huge boost to your development.

Just as you want your players to see the best possible demonstration of a skill during a practice session, make sure you watch coaches who will provide a useful example. Ideally you should try to observe more experienced coaches who are working with players of a similar level to you.

It is also useful to watch the next age group up from yours, and to watch junior performance squads (county and district) to gain an understanding of what players and coaching sessions look like at the next level up.

Take a coaching course or workshop

The England and Wales Cricket Board (ECB) offers a range of different coach education courses. Many people who read this book will already have a qualification, but there are courses available for coaches at all different levels of experience. These range from workshops lasting a few hours, to qualifications that take several days and a considerable amount of observed coaching in between.

To learn more about the ECB's coaching pathway visit http://www.ecb.co.uk/development/coach-education/ or contact your local cricket board – every county has one.

In addition to the ECB courses, many counties will run informal workshops throughout the year. These usually involve prominent coaches running sessions on specific areas of the game, such as developing fast bowlers or teaching batsmen how to play spin. Contact your local cricket board or coaches association for details.

Resources/ECB Coaches Association

The ECB Coaches Association (ECBCA) provides excellent support and resources for qualified coaches. From £30 a year (at the time of writing), membership gives you access to a wide range of benefits and resources to help you in your coaching. These include regular coaching DVDs and magazines full of new ideas, and the latest up-to-date coaching methods.

Another useful ECB resource is its groundbreaking Howzat! computer software. This is now given to everyone attending a 'Coaching Children' or 'Coaching Young People and Adults' coaching course. It contains practices, videos and information on the player development model, and is well worth checking out.

Coaching Kit

There is an increasingly wide range of equipment available to enhance your coaching sessions. Below is a brief guide to some of the main items you might want to consider having in your coaching kit bag. ECBCA members can access discounted kit through the ECB website, but to make sure you get the best prices shop around on line.

Essentials

Balls

A large supply of balls is vital for running any coaching session. There are many different types available, and the number and variety of balls you need will depend on the age group you are working with.

Tennis balls: These are useful for any age, and the more you have the better. A good way of getting hold of tennis balls is to make contact with your local tennis club. They will often discard used balls, but these are still perfect for cricket practices. If you are lucky they may even donate them for free!

Incrediballs or **windballs:** In addition to tennis balls it is advisable to have a half dozen incrediballs or windballs. These are rubber balls with a seam, and are great for bowling and fielding practices. They are also useful in the transition between softball and hardball cricket.

Cricket balls: These are like gold dust for coaches and seem to have a habit of disappearing, so it is a good idea to count them out and count them in at the start and end of each session. Ideally you should have balls of different ages – that is, some new balls, some a few overs old, and a few older ones. Cricket balls are expensive, but you should avoid buying really cheap ones as they can damage bats and won't last.

Make sure that you hang on to any balls used in matches, and put them in your kitbag afterwards. For the players we are looking at coaching in this book (under thirteen) you need junior size balls (4¾oz). Giving your young bowlers full size balls to practice with can have a detrimental effect, particularly for spin bowlers.

Bowling machine balls: If you are doing a lot of batting practices with hard balls it is also useful to have a supply of bowling machine balls. These are harder wearing than cricket balls but bounce in a similar way. However, they should not be used for bowling.

Stumps

There are a number of different types of stumps available to coaches, from the traditional wooden ones used in matches to lightweight foam ones. Which ones you use is likely to depend on what you are using them for, and your budget. Ideally you want about four sets of stumps, and this may include a mixture of different types.

For durability and value for money your best bet are the plastic stumps which fit into a plastic base. These are fairly lightweight and virtually impossible to break, which means they can be used with hard or soft balls. You can use them in nets, indoors and on grass, and they give you the option of having one, two or three stumps at a time. The only down side is that they can be blown over in the wind, and the base gives players a slightly unrealistic target to aim at.

At the other end of the price range you have foam stumps. These can now be fitted into a base or used individually. They are lightweight, easy to carry around, and are particularly good for fielding practices.

Other options include spring-back stumps, which are good for nets but heavy and unwieldy, and wooden fielding stumps which are mounted on a spring. In my experience these are prone to break, and they have a large metal spike on the bottom which is not entirely safe when used with children.

Cones and markers

Cones and markers are an essential piece of kit. The best are the small circular ones with a hole in the top, as they are easy to carry and can double up as batting tees. They come in sets, and are cheap and readily available. One set should be sufficient, but it never hurts to have more.

As well as these small cones there are a number of other types available, from traffic cone shapes to half spherical ones. However, the best ones to get are the flat rubber markers that come in a variety of shapes and sizes. These are great because they are visual but do not cause the ball to deviate much if it hits them. Therefore they are good to use for batting practices where the feeder requires a target to aim for, and for target bowling. They can also be used to show players where to put their feet for a certain skill.

Batting tees

The last essential for a coach of young players are batting tees. These are really useful when teaching basic batting shots to beginners, and are available from all cricket coaching equipment retailers.

The best ones to get are the more rigid plastic ones as they last longer than the soft rubber ones, which can bend and warp in your bag. Tees may seem relatively expensive but are an investment well worth making. If you are on a low budget then the throwaway plastic cups you get from the supermarket are a decent substitute, but they will break easily and can't be balanced on a stump for pull shot practices.

Additional items

There are any number of other coaching aids and pieces of kit available these days. Your club or school should be able to step in and help with the more expensive items that can be used across age groups, but here are a couple more items it may be useful to have in your personal kit bag.

Baseball mitt

For most modern-day coaches a baseball mitt has become an indispensable part of their kit. They allow you to run hard-ball fielding practices and bowling drills at full pace without worrying about safety. As most squads will only have one or two wicketkeepers it gives you the flexibility to run extra groups. If you have never used one before they may take a while to get used to, but it is well worth taking the time to master. If you are right-handed you will need a left-handed glove, and vice versa.

Although you can get cheap mitts it is worth spending more to get a proper leather one as they have more padding and will last longer.

Fielding bat

If you are a decent hitter you may be able to get away with using a full size bat, but for most coaches it is easier to hit catches using a specialized fielding bat. These shorter bats are available from most cricket retailers and come in two main styles.

The cheaper option is basically a scaled-down version of a normal bat. They have the benefit of sounding and reacting like a real bat, but can take a bit of getting used to before you can hit consistently.

The other option is a similarly scaled-down bat with a foam rubber face; it is slightly heavier than the purely wooden alternative. These are easier to hit with and require much less timing or power. However, they do not sound or react like real bats, which means that an element of realism can be lost from the practice. They are also significantly more expensive.

Other items that are worth considering are katchet boards, mini-football goals, foam targets and balance boards/cushions.

Katchet boards: These are plastic squares with ridges on that are mainly used in fielding practices. The ridges mean that when a ball is thrown at them it will bounce off in a fairly unpredictable way, which is great for close-catching and flat-catching drills.

Mini football goals: These make a good target for batsmen to aim at, and can be placed behind the stumps to stop balls during fielding practices. They are lightweight and come in a variety of sizes.

Foam targets: These can be placed on top of the stumps to give bowlers a visual aid. However, it is possible to make something similar yourself, or to use a ball on top of a tee as an alternative.

Balance boards/cushions: These are good when helping young players establish a strong base for batting or fielding. They also improve balance and core strength.

Technology

Technology has long been a part of cricket at élite level, and increasingly some of the gadgets and gizmos that were previously only available to professionals can now be used at grass roots level.

Video analysis

Video analysis is a useful tool for coaches as it allows you to see things you might miss with the naked eye. Just as when you are observing your players normally, think what angles you need to video from, and make sure you can do it safely and without interfering with the practice.

As well as capturing footage using a video camera you can also film players on tablets and smart phones. One of the best apps I have come across for this is Cricket Coach Plus HD, which can be downloaded for just £1.99 (at the time of writing). The program allows you to watch players in slow motion, annotate footage, and to compare this with footage of a technical model.

Note: If using video footage, make sure you share it with your players, and beware of 'paralysis by analysis'. A video is likely to show up flaws in technique you may not otherwise notice, but that does not mean you have to flag them all up with your player. Just as when analysing in a normal practice, try to focus on the one or two key points that are most relevant to your player.

Scoring apps

In recent years a number of electronic scoring apps has come on to the market. These not only aid scorers, but allow you to access a wide range of statistical data on your players' performance in matches, which was previously reserved for professionals. As well as scoring games, they produce features such as feature wagon wheels, pitch maps and run rate graphs which offer a real insight into the performance of your players both individually and as a team. Popular apps include CricHQ, Total Cricket Scorer and NXcricket-HD.

ECB GUIDELINES

The pitch

A standard cricket pitch is 22 yards long (20.12m), but younger players use shorter strips.

According to ECB guidelines an under sevens pitch should be 16 yards, an under wicket should be 18 yards and an under ten strip 19 yards long. Under elevens should play over 20 yards, while an under thirteen strip is 21 yards long. From under 14s upwards players use a full size pitch.

All of the above distances relate to cricket played with a hard ball. If you are using a softer ball, e.g. a rubber ball, then the distances should be reduced. A rough guide for distances when using a softer ball is; 14 yards for under sevens, 15 yards for under nines, 16 yards for under elevens.

Stumps

It is recommended that junior cricket up to and including under thirteens should be played with stumps measuring 27 × 8 inches. From under fourteen upwards full size stumps are used (28 × 9 inches).

The ball

All age groups from under thirteens down, playing with a hard ball should use a smaller ball weighing 4.75 oz. From under fourteen upwards, players use a full size ball; 5.5 oz for boys and 5oz for girls.

ECB fielding restrictions

According to ECB fielding regulations no player aged fifteen or under should field closer than eight yards from the middle stump at the batting end. If they are under thirteen the distance is 10 metres. These distances do not apply if the fielder is behind the wicket on the off side. Any player under the age of eighteen fielding within 5.5m of the bat must wear a helmet and abdominal protector (boys).

ECB fast bowling directives

In order to protect young players from injury the ECB has provided directives limiting the number of overs a fast bowler may bowl in both a single spell and in a day.

Players in the under thirteen age group and below the maximum number of overs a fast bowler may bowl in a spell is five, with no more than ten to be bowled in a day.

For under fourteens and fifteens the directives allow for six over spells and a maximum of twelve per day. Under sixteens and seventeens can bowl seven over spells and eighteen per day.

For these purposes a 'fast bowler' is defined as a bowler for whom a wicketkeeper in the same age group would normally stand back to take the ball.

INDEX

back foot defence 58–59
back foot drive 55–56,
batting 45–68
  backswing 47
  grip 45–46
  introducing a hard ball 68
  mental and physical drill 66–67
  practices 51–68
  stance 46
bowling 69–84
  away swing 82
  follow through 70
  grips 70–72, 82–83
  in swing 82
  off spin 71–72
  release 70
  run-up 69
  take off 69
bowling practices
  bowl off 75–76
  bowling at the death 77–79
  bowling corridor 76–77
  flight practice 80–81
  hit the cones 77–78
  leg spin practice 80
  off spin practice 79
  target bowling 74–75
  traffic lights 81–82

catching 86–91, 111–112
close catch 86–87, 111–112
coaching courses 136–137
coaching during a match 133–135
coaching kit and equipment 137–140
  balls 137–138, 141
  batting tees 138
  stumps/wickets 138, 141
  technology 139–140
coaching on match days 132–135
coaching philosophy 28
coaching post-match 135
coaching tools 14–27, 126

coach-to -player ratios 37
continuum of practice 37–38
cool down 126–127, 135
crow-hop 99–101

demonstrations 16–20
  live 18
  player 19
  shadow 18
development vs winning 129–130
differentiation 127–128
dynamic stretching 39–43

ECB Coaches Association 136
ECB fast bowling directives 141
ECB fielding restrictions 141
encouraging self-reflection 114, 126

feeding for batting 47–51, 128
  bobble feeds 50–51
  drop feeds 48–50
  full toss feeds 50
  hitting off a tee 47–48
  overarm feeds 51
fielding 85–101, 108–114
fielding positions 85
  boundary fielders 85–86
  close catchers 85
  ring fielders 85
front foot defence 57–58
front foot drive 51–53, 66–67,
  118–119

games 11, 115–120, 132–135
  coaching games 120
  diamond cricket 117–118
  front foot drive shoot out 118–119
  non-stop cricket 116–117
  pairs cricket 115–116
  pairs cricket conditioned game
    119–120
giving instructions 14–15, 17

high catch 87–89, 108, 111–112
hitting gaps 64–66
hitting over the top 63

leg spin 72
Long Term Athlete Development Model 29–30
    FUNdamentals 29
    Learning to Train 29
    Training to Train 29–30

making a practice fun 34
middle practices 123

nets 121–124
    match scenarios: the middle of an innings
        122–123
    match scenarios: opening up 122
    match scenarios: the end of an innings 123
    physical net: 123–124
    when you are out you are out 121–122
non-stop cricket 11, 116–118

observing and analysing players 20–23
off spin 71–72
one hand intercept and underarm throw 94–96,
    109–111
overarm throw 91–93

pairs cricket 115–116, 119–120
parents 130
pitch length 141
Player Development Model 30
player discipline and dealing with difficult behaviour
    130–132
player roles 130
player-centred coaching 7–13
    player-centred approach in practice 11–12
playing spin 61–63
praising players 35
pre-delivery movements 47
pre-match preparation 132–133
providing feedback 22, 24–26
pull shot 53–55

questioning 25–27

ready position 94
risk assessment 36
running a team 129

safety 36
seam bowling 69–71, 75–79,
    83–4
    alignment 70, 76–77
    practices 74–82
seam movement 83
self reflection 133
session planning 37, 125–126
skim catch 89–91, 111–112
spin bowling 69–77, 79–82
    introducing spin 74
    practices 74–82
square cut 59–61
swing bowling 82–83

taking quick singles 62–64
team fielding drills 109–114
    around the stumps 112–113
    ground fielding triangle 109–110
    one hand intercept square
        110–111
    three line catching challenge
        111–112
    working in pairs 113–114
technical model 33
throw downs 133
throwing 91–100, 109–110, 112–114
turn and throw 96–99
two handed pick-up and crow-hop 99–101,
    109–110, 112–113

Under 9 key skills 30–31
Under 11 key skills 31–32
Under 13 key skills 32
using this book 38

walking in 94
warm-ups 39–43, 132–133
    batting relay 40–41
    bowling warm-up 42–43
    dynamic stretch circle 43–44
    dynamic tag 41
    hand hockey 39
what next 136–137
wicketkeeping 85, 101–107, 109
    catching edges 107
    stance 102
    standing back 102–104
    standing up 102, 104–106

OTHER SPORTS TITLES
FROM CROWOOD

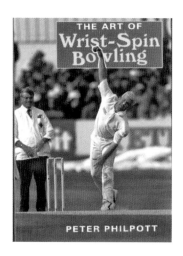

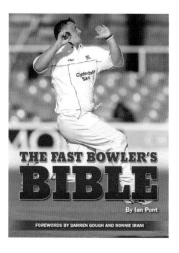

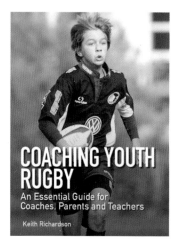

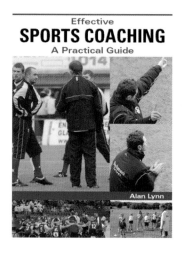